CH   Lu

GW00469672

BRIEF SWEET LIFE

First edition
published in 2005 by

WOODFIELD PUBLISHING
Bognor Regis, West Sussex, England
www.woodfieldpublishing.com

ISBN 1-903953-79-0

Brief Sweet Life

This is their legacy…this is their story…

GLEN ROSE

Woodfield

The first crew at RAF Silverstone. No.17 OTU in 1943.
From left to right Back row Duncan and Ben. Front row: Ted, Chas and Ginger

Contents

Chapter One..1

Chapter Two..8

Chapter Three..12

Chapter Four..19

Chapter Five...24

Chapter Six...29

Chapter Seven..33

Chapter Eight...40

Chapter Nine..45

Chapter Ten..49

Chapter Eleven...56

Chapter Twelve..62

Chapter Thirteen...69

Chapter Fourteen..74

Chapter Fifteen..81

Chapter Sixteen...84

Chapter Seventeen..89

Chapter Eighteen..95

Chapter Nineteen..100

Chapter Twenty 107

Chapter Twenty One 110

Chapter Twenty Two 118

Chapter Twenty Three 126

Chapter Twenty Four 137

Chapter Twenty Five 141

Chapter Twenty Six 150

Chapter Twenty Seven 155

Chapter Twenty Eight 160

Chapter Twenty Nine 163

Epilogue 167

Epitaph 178

Bibliography & Acknowledgements 179

Photographs 180

Introduction

Flak was everywhere around them now; streams of tracer fire danced by like rivers of light; blood-red flashes and angry rays of brilliant light leaping everywhere without warning. The very air around them was crackling. Then he saw the searchlights. Cruel shafts of intense brilliance, scything at the sky around their aircraft, trying to capture it, trap it, ready for the kill. Seconds later came the deafening burst of heavy shells. It was at that moment that they were coned. The darkness inside the aircraft was flooded with a blinding blue-white light that scorched their eyes. They were trapped. It was the end. Twenty massive searchlight beams pinned them to the sky. It would be only a matter of seconds before the flak guns followed the beams and their aircraft would become a massive ball of incandescent flame.

I looked at my father's face, strained and twisted with pain. His eyes seemed to look beyond me, to the past.

"Another headache, Dad?" I enquired gently.

He'd had so many of them recently. The doctor said they were a symptom of post-traumatic stress and assured me that it could come on many years later. It was sixty or more years ago now. I knew what had brought it all on of course. He'd been looking through some old photograph albums that had stirred up the memories. Memories – long hidden, long buried. Painful memories. So painful that just the thought of them brought on those dreadful headaches.

I sat down to talk to him about the past, to help him to unburden himself and maybe, finally, come to terms with it.

He began by talking to me first about Agnes…

CHAPTER ONE

Agnes was the mother of my father. I never knew her, but I can tell you that she was very beautiful. I know that because I once made a pencil drawing of her from an old sepia photo. Every curve of her lovely face, every soft tendril of her hair seemed familiar to me, yet I never knew her.

Agnes died when my father was a boy – just fourteen – a vulnerable age. He loved her dearly and her loss through heart failure was a tragedy in his young life, especially so because his father, Eddie, was a hard, cold man who could be cruel to his three children. Eddie had an eye for the ladies and Agnes's death stopped him in his self-righteous march through life for barely a heartbeat. He married Ida just a few short weeks after Agnes died and she assumed the rôle of mother to Agnes's three children, though in their eyes she was little more than a usurper. The union produced three more children and the little terraced house in Manchester would become even more unbearable for my father – the middle child of Agnes's innocent trinity.

Agnes's eldest, a girl, was a sassy miss who wore her hats at a jaunty angle and learned how to get Eddie round to her way of thinking. Agnes's youngest was a rosy-cheeked boy who never stopped trying to be the apple of his father's eye. But my father, Agnes's middle child, Duncan, was a gentle lad, full of strength and loyalty, who loved his mother with all his young heart.

Times were hard and the acquisition of a high school education was a luxury forbidden to Agnes's middle child. Forced to leave school at the tender age of fourteen in order to bring home a wage, Duncan had been sent to work for Manchester Corporation's Housing Department. Eddie's brother, Jack, was a foreman and had pulled a few strings in his nephew's favour. So, clad in his denim bib and brace overalls, the young joiner's apprentice mounted his bicycle at half past seven each morning and pedalled the seven long miles from the red brick terraces of Levenshulme to the embryonic, model housing estates of Wythenshawe in rural south Manchester.

The bicycle – a Hercules – had cost Eddie a resentful three pounds, nineteen shillings and eleven pence. Duncan had wanted a Raleigh, but at five pounds, the illustrious item was not for the likes of him. Nonetheless, he was immensely proud of his new bike (in the way that fourteen year old boys are) and struggling, had carried it up the twisting stairs to show to his beloved mother as she lay in her sick bed. She had smiled at him, her gentle features lighting up as she looked with pride at her young son, on his way to manhood. She knew her days would be short and she hoped she might prepare him, warn him so that he could be strong. Taking his tanned and sturdy hand in her fragile grasp, she pressed his fingers to her chest and whispered "Just feel my heart, son". She was so thin, so frail. He could feel her heart fluttering fast. He knew then. And so it was, in the late summer of 1935, just a few weeks after his fourteenth birthday, that Duncan began his working life. In the early autumn, just as the leaves began to fall, Agnes died. Summoned from work by an urgent telephone call, Duncan rode the seven miles home on the longest journey he would ever make on his Hercules bicycle.

Workdays became a temporary distraction through the sad and lonely autumn and winter that followed. At the Benchill Farm Office, Duncan and his fellow joiner's apprentices worked hard under the watchful eye of foreman Billy Andrews, an angry red-faced man whose tumultuous outbursts earned him a shortened, unhealthy life. With sharpened pencils the boys carefully marked the wood then cut it to size. An apprentice's first set of tools was a source of pride to be lovingly tended: hammer, axe, saw and plugging chisel all neatly stored in a nailbag, complete with a two foot rule and a joiner's pencil. Billy Bains, Duncan's fellow apprentice, spent all his spare time meticulously cleaning and shining his tools. In today's psycho-soaked society he would probably be termed a compulsive obsessive and offered counselling, but back then he was grudgingly admired. Not only his tools, but also his boots, enjoyed the benefit of Billy's mental obsession; for young Billy Bains had the cleanest, shiniest boots of all the employees in the entire Manchester Corporation. Duncan took care not to stand too close to Billy lest his own mean boots – their holed soles patched with stout cardboard – be drawn into unfair comparison. Duncan had to hand over his weekly wage of twelve shillings and sixpence to Eddie – and the two shillings and sixpence he was given back for himself would not cover the cost of new shoe leather.

In the colder months the lads looked forward to putting the kettle onto the fire and warming their chilled hands, ready to make the tea. Out from their hessian nail bags would come the newspaper twists filled with tea leaves, sugar and a thick dollop of oversweet, condensed milk. This nectar would be carefully scraped from its newsprint platter into a tannin-stained brew can, ready to be drowned in freshly boiled water. Toasted cheese over an open wood fire was a rare treat that made the half hour break worth looking forward to.

In the spring, as the sun began to set later, the working day finished at five instead of four thirty. To compensate, dinner time was a full hour from twelve till one, but Duncan had always eaten his sandwiches by then so as to have the full hour free for his own explorations. When the foreman blew the twelve o'clock whistle, Duncan would jump on his bike, briefly stop at the mobile shop on the corner for a two-penny Cadbury's chocolate bar, and pedal furiously off down Woodhouse Road for the ten minute ride out to Ringway.

Work on Ringway aerodrome had begun in the late 1920s in the leafy Cheshire lanes at Rackhouse Park, Wythenshawe, to serve the city of Manchester. Wythenshawe at that time would be totally unrecognisable to today's inhabitants of the area. It was largely undeveloped, being instead a delightful pastoral backwater – in sharp contrast to the concrete jungle it was to become when modernisation, in the shape of the model council estates being built by Manchester Corporation, had finally gobbled up all the green and pleasant land. The planners euphemistically called their fine development a "Garden City" – perhaps hoping to be fondly remembered as the Titus Salts or George Cadburys of their day, but the inhabitants of Wythenshawe would soon know it to be otherwise. Created to house the overspill from the inner city slums, Wythenshawe soon became a vast, sprawling, council estate full of little boxes.

But before the war things were different in those country lanes, as Duncan pedalled along them to watch the aeroplanes out at Ringway. The aerodrome was undergoing expansion and almost six hundred and fifty acres of land had been acquired for the buildings and runways. It was an exciting place for the young joiner's apprentice, far removed from his daily rote of pencils, hammers and saws. Duncan was fascinated by the magic of flight. When he had been a young schoolboy, he and his friends had spent many precious days of their school holidays on the open land out at Highfield Road watching the Barnstormers. This was the Golden Age of Aviation – the peaceful years that followed the agonies of the First World War. A time to gasp for breath before the storm clouds gathered again. A time to experiment and develop. A time to reflect.

Manchester was no stranger to aviation history. The first long distance flight in England had been in April, 1910, when the French exhibition pilot, Louis Paulhan landed his Farman bi-plane in a field next to Burnage Station, just a few miles from Duncan's home in nearby Levenshulme. In doing so, Paulhan had claimed the £10,000 Daily Mail prize for the London to Manchester race and became the first person to fly the 186 miles in under twenty-four hours. As he had come in to land, Paulhan had delighted and amazed the incredulous crowd by waving at them excitedly from his open cockpit, his eyes searching for his pretty wife and pet black poodle amongst the waiting throng.

A desire to fly, to see the earth as a patchwork quilt, to soar high into the clouds; this was Duncan's dream. As a young lad he used to revel in the picture story strips of air adventures that were in his weekly comics. He was lucky, for only a few of his friends got comics each week, but because Eddie had a daily paper, he allowed his two eldest children a weekly comic too – sometimes it was the Wizard and sometimes the Hotspur. Every Saturday morning Duncan would spend his entire tuppence pocket money on a matinee performance at the nearby Arcadia cinema. He especially enjoyed Hells Angels, an action film about the First World War that made heroes of the brave pilots and gunners. The bi-planes that look so ancient to our twenty first century eyes were like futuristic dream machines right out of a science fiction comic to the little lads on the tuppeny seats in the Arcadia.

The first time that Duncan saw a bi-plane in real life was forever etched on his memory. Eddie had sent him on an errand to fill a jug of beer at the off-licence near the hay field alongside Highfield Road. Duncan carried the empty jug past the poor cottages that crouched down low on Craddock Fold where his old adversary Mark Beresford lived. The pair held a mutual dislike for each other and had fought hard, each bloodying the other's nose. They had shaken hands afterwards, each boy deciding independently that enough was enough, but Duncan couldn't be sure that Beresford wouldn't have had a change of heart. He scurried past the cottages with their wooden steps, clutching the earthenware jug tightly, knowing that he would get a good hiding if he dropped it. Past the UCP tripe factory with its warm and distinctive odour, past the carpet factory with its lumbering cart horses hauling the bundles of jute, and on to the shop on the parade where he would buy the beer for his dad.

It was the noise that caught his attention first, a droning unlike any other sound he knew. When it stopped, he heard the squeals of excitement and as curiosity got the better of him, he kicked up his heels and ran past the shops and round the corner to see what was going on.

In the hay field was a bi-plane – a Tiger Moth – surrounded by a group of people including a number of excited children. The pilot clambered out, unfastening his flying helmet and walked over to a small group of overalled mechanics who were stood outside the larger of two tents. A rope fence had been erected to mark off the take-off and landing area, and just outside the ropes was a brightly coloured poster announcing the arrival of "Colonel Cody's Flying Circus". Duncan recognised one of the bystanders in the crowd, an old man called Mr. Moody who used to lodge at Eddie's house. He went over and asked him if he knew what was going on.

"It's the Barnstormers, they're taking people up for trips but it costs five shillings" wheezed Mr. Moody. "Five bob . . . . . " his yellow eyes held Duncan's excited gaze and he paused for effect, puffing quietly on his briar pipe. Five shillings was a fortune to a young lad who had just tuppence pocket money a week. Only a rich man or a fool could afford that – but there were plenty of both in Manchester. The Barnstormers gave rides and flying lessons to those with money in their pockets, and when the supply of rich men and fools in Manchester ran out, they moved their flying circus on to the next town.

Oh, if only he had five shillings. Duncan watched the bi-plane gathering speed along the bumpy ground, its propellers straining and churning round and round. Then, as his heart beat fit to burst and he knew the aeroplane was about to crash into the trees, its nose went up and it soared into the blue sky. In his excitement Duncan tightened his grip on the beer jug – the feel of its familiar shape brought him back to earth with a jolt. He'd be late with the beer, he'd be in trouble. He ran as fast as he dared back to the shop, carrying with him the empty jug and the exhilarating memory of the soaring bi-plane. One day. One day. He was going to get his feet off the ground – he was going to fly.

CHAPTER TWO

Ringway wasn't Manchester's first choice for an airport. The Municipal Corporation had wanted the kudos of having one of the first civic aerodromes in the country and they began by putting their money into Barton, an area of open land to the west of Manchester city centre near the River Mersey and the Victorian engineering miracle known as the Manchester Ship Canal. The land at Foxhill Farm on Barton Moss was already owned by the Corporation's Cleansing department and typical Lancashire thrift was paramount in the decision to develop the sixty acres of mossland into Barton Airport. Thus in 1929, Barton became the first municipal airfield in the UK to be licensed by the Air Ministry. The downward spiralling fate of the new airport was sealed, however, by its location and terrain, the clue to its demise being found in the word "Moss" in the area's name, for *mos* is old English denoting an area of swamp or bog.

Barton Moss is a product of the last Ice Age. An area of low lying and poorly drained peat bog, it lies on the edge of the larger Chat Moss, an area that has proved a major challenge to transportation many times in the past. In the early 1800s, George Stephenson's radical idea to run the Manchester to Liverpool Railway across the mossland had been met with both ridicule and astonishment. Flying in the face of his detractors who called the idea a "perfect madness", Stephenson first ran a four mile heather footpath across the bog, marking out the route. Then a floating, pliable raft was made of timber, moss, heather and brushwood hurdles. A narrow rail line was laid on top of it and the railroad became a reality. Clinker and ash from the local power station were the preferred foundations for Barton airport, however, but other factors also weighed in to doom its rise to fame. Not only was the runway too small for the increasing size of the airliners but the micro climate of the low lying land was the final nail in Barton's coffin. Heavy mists known as fern fogs produce a dense layer that affects visibility – so essential for aircraft when taking off and landing. Ringway being some forty feet higher above sea level, was not affected by mists in the same way. So development at Ringway got the green light.

In 1934 the Fairey Aviation Company had taken over a former First World War factory at Heaton Chapel, near Stockport, just a few miles from Ringway. Here they began producing the Fairey Battle aircraft for the RAF, to replace the old, and now obsolete, bi-planes. As the buds began to swell and open in the first fresh days of spring, 1936, the initial test flights of the Battle began at Barton. Within weeks however, the test flying was transferred to the up and coming Ringway, and Duncan's daily bike rides to the airport took on a far more fascinating aspect. The airport buildings were little more than a few hangars and a group of wooden huts, but the long runway and apron were all that mattered – were all that was needed.

The Fairey Battle was an impressive looking machine compared to the old Barnstormer bi-planes that had given such thrills to the impressionable children (and adult passengers) at the Highfield Road hay field. A single-engine, low wing monoplane; the light bomber boasted sleek lines topped off with the distinctive RAF roundel that showed brightly against the dark grey, metal skin. Duncan pedalled hard past the old smithy in Crossacres, turned right onto Ringway Road and then bumped along the cinder path that led to an area overlooking the apron where the aircraft were parked. His heart beat a tattoo in his chest as he prayed that one of them would take off during the precious half hour that he could stay.

The air crew fascinated Duncan as he watched them walking around the planes, clad in fancy flying boots and fur lined leather jackets. A flying helmet and goggles completed the prestigious, man-of-action kit – a world away from his own apprentice's shabby overalls. As he watched, the three crew members, pilot, navigator and wireless operator/gunner, climbed into one of the aircraft and settled down into the "greenhouse" – the glazed cockpit and crew section from where the instruments and two machine guns were operated. It seemed forever, yet was only minutes, before the three-bladed propeller that was mounted on the nose cone rent the air and the Rolls-Royce Merlin engine roared into life. The flight mechanics unplugged the accumulator battery from the side of the plane and quickly wheeled it away, steering a wide berth around the thrashing propeller. The Battle inched forward, lurching a little, gathered speed and taxied off toward the end of the runway ready for take-off.

The excitement amongst the onlookers was palpable as the aeroplane rushed down the runway toward them on its test flight. Although you knew, just knew, it would take off alright, no-one could really be certain until physical contact between the ground and the plane was broken and the aircraft was surging forward and, more importantly, upward. The runway ended a few hundred yards inside the airport perimeter, an ear splitting "stone's throw" from where Duncan and his fellow air-enthusiasts were standing. The plane speeded towards them and then, at the last minute soared skyward over their heads, with a terrifying roar. Watching, gasping, shouting in awe – Duncan felt as if his heart had stopped – the exhilaration was like an electric shock. His head strained upward, eyes narrowing against the brightness of the midday sun, following the path of the plane. Smaller and smaller, silhouetted against the sky, the pilot executed a neat turn and the plane banked gently to make a circuit over the green

Cheshire countryside. Watching its course intently, Duncan was spellbound, longing with all his being to be inside the plane – clad in flying helmet and goggles – flying higher, ever higher. He was brought back to earth with a bump as one of the nearby spectators gave him a gentle nudge.

"Don't you have to be back at work soon, son?"

Duncan pulled out his old pocket watch – it was quarter to one. "Thanks, yes, yes" he mumbled. Duncan was both grateful to his fellow onlooker for saving him from the catalogue of awful problems that would follow if he was late for work, yet was also frustrated at having to leave this blissful place of dreams.

He mounted his Hercules bike and pedalled away furiously, glancing over his shoulder to watch the plane still circling overhead. The Fairey Battle continued its test flight, one of many more to follow. But far fiercer and crueller tests lay ahead – for the intrepid Battle was to take over the RAF's light bomber rôle in the early war years to come. Its vulnerability would be exposed quickly – it was too slow and under-gunned – and the German *Luftwaffe* fighter attacks would soon ravage the unescorted Battle formations. Four years after that sunny spring day at Ringway, almost half the available Fairey Battles stationed in France would be lost in just one day, sacrificed to the speed and surprise of the advancing German *Blitzkreig*.

But those days were in the future, for the drums of war were beating only gently that spring day in 1936.

CHAPTER THREE

Len O'Donnell was Duncan's best friend. They lived five doors apart on the same street in Levenshulme and had been pals since they were little lads. Despite many differences in outlook and ability, they stuck together until a girl came on the scene. But then to be fair, she was no ordinary girl. With her creamy skin, perfect mouth, soft brown hair and mesmerising green-grey eyes, she was vivacious enough to attract most of the young men in the neighbourhood. She stood out from all the other pretty girls because of her self-confident aura that was underlined by a unique sense of style. It was the mid 1930s, times were hard, money was short, and few young women were able to indulge themselves with clothes or cosmetics. But this girl had a way of making anything look good, it was the panache and pizzazz with which she wore her clothes and the way she carried herself. If she'd been dressed in a sack she would still have looked chic.

Duncan and Len had been at school together (though in different classes) but while Duncan went to train as an apprentice joiner, Len had started out as an apprentice engineer at Herbert's, making tank gearing. At the weekends they met up again as they both played for the Green Bank Rangers football team whose home ground was at the local Errwood Park. On Sundays they went their separate ways as each lad was in a different church choir (Len was in St Mark's and Duncan attended St. Peter's) but they would usually meet up after church, if family matters didn't intervene. One Sunday in August 1937, Len had told Duncan to meet him after church by the shops on Byron Parade, hinting that he might bring a couple of friends along. And so it was that balmy summer evening, as Duncan stood waiting for his friend, that he first set eyes on Pauline.

She was beautiful; exquisite. He was captivated by her gentle smile and her enigmatic eyes – green one moment, blue-grey the next. She turned her gaze upward to meet his and he fell in love so hard that it was like a physical pain. She looked at him, standing tall, with twinkling, soft brown eyes and dark, wavy hair, and she too, fell in love (though almost seventy years would pass before she would at last confess that she began to love him on that long-ago August day).

The summer turned to autumn, and Pauline would see him at the weekends as she and her friend Effie went to watch the local lads play football. Duncan would watch for her in the crowd and try to catch her eye and smile in her direction. Sometimes she'd be huddled under an umbrella as the rain poured down. And he'd wave at her, feeling embarrassed at his muddy clothes and sodden appearance, but the smile she returned warmed him more than the summer sun. When the blizzards came in December he was frustrated as the matches were called off and everyone stayed indoors seeking warmth.

Winter turned to spring and then summer. At seventeen, Duncan felt more assured and was determined to ask Pauline to go out with him. He confided in his friend Len.

"Nice try," said Len, "but Pauline's already courting." Len smiled as Duncan's face dropped.

"But, she never said... I, I didn't know. Why? I mean... who?" Duncan faltered over his question, looking quizzically at Len.

The answer took Duncan's breath away.

"Me. I'm going out with Pauline," smirked Len.

Duncan's discomfiture would have been painful to watch for anyone other than Len, who merely smiled again and nodded a further, un-necessary confirmation. He knew that Duncan was his loyal pal and would never transgress their long standing friendship by approaching Pauline. And of course he was right.

Duncan's loneliness was profound – the recent loss of his mother remained a mantle of thorns that he wore each day. Just when he had begun to hope that sweetness might again enter into his life, his dreams had been dashed. Anxiety replaced hope.

Anxiety was a frequent state of mind that summer and autumn, not just for Duncan, but for most of the British populace. Rumours of German military movement in Europe were met by appeasement and cries of "negotiation, negotiation". On a gentle September morning, Neville Chamberlain stepped on board a plane for the very first time in his life and flew to meet Adolf Hitler at the secluded, Alpine mountain retreat at Berchtesgaden. He returned to Britain saying that he believed Hitler to be a man who could be relied upon when he had given his word. A few short weeks later, Chamberlain's words "Peace in our time" were on everyone's lips. Hope replaced anxiety.

Though Duncan accepted that Pauline had chosen Len, he couldn't get her out of his mind. He altered his route to and from work so as to ride by her house – for the advantage of seeing her far outweighed the disadvantage that she might glimpse him in his workman's overalls. He went to as many of the social events that he thought she might attend, but he was frustrated by jealousy each Sunday as he walked to church. The distinctive stone-work of St Peter's beckoned, as Duncan ran ahead of the rest of his family so as to don his choir member's surplice and cassock. As he took his place at the back of the church ready to proceed up the aisle with the choir, he watched the congregation filing in to take their places on the hard, wooden pews. He spotted the familiar figure of his father, resplendent in his dandified Sunday best, complete with shiny topped cane. Len would be at his own church, St Mark's, by now, and **he** would have the joy of seeing Pauline walking by with her family, no doubt bestowing a beautiful smile on him. Duncan watched the minister settling in at the pulpit and as he began the slow, swaying, rhythmic progression to the front of the church, singing the first of the morning's anthems, his mind was full of torment.

If Duncan had had even an inkling of what he was about to learn later that morning, his face would not have been so miserable nor his heart so heavy. The previous evening a group of young things had gone to the cinema to watch a Laurel and Hardy film called "Way Out West". Pauline was part of the group and she teamed up with two of the young men, Reg and Arthur, as they all left the cinema in the dark October night. Pauline was obviously about to walk home by herself, so Arthur chivalrously volunteered both his and Reg's services as escorts. Pauline smiled her thanks, but she was completely taken by surprise to hear Reg ask:

"Why are you on your own, Pauline? I thought you were going out with Len O'Donnell?"

Pauline was indignant. "I most certainly am not!" she replied emphatically, "I'm not going out with **anyone!**"

The two young men exchanged glances full of unspoken words. Their pal Duncan would be the next to know the news.

The church service seemed ponderously slow that Sunday morning, and the starched white ruff seemed even more uncomfortable. Duncan fingered it irritably, trying to ease the itching it was causing on the back of his neck. Finally it was over, and in the sanctuary of the choir changing room he gratefully removed the offending garment and shrugged into his Sunday best jacket. Leaving the heavy, incense laden atmosphere of the church, Duncan gulped in the crisp October morning air. As he stood quietly contemplating the loneliness of the day ahead, he felt two rough arms – one on either side – grasp him and steer him out through the lych gate and onto the street.

"Dunc" said Arthur on his right "we've got something to tell you".

"Yes" said Reg on his left "just wait till you hear what we found out last night".

"What?" demanded Duncan.

"Well, you know how you told us that Len O'Donnell was courting that girl you took a shine to…"

"You mean Pauline?" said Duncan. "Go on – what about it?" he demanded.

"We saw her last night at the flicks and she was by herself," revealed Reg.

"And more than that Dunc," Arthur joined in. "We asked her where Len was because we'd heard that the two of them were an item. Anyway, you should have seen her face when we told her that we thought she was going out with Len. She was really mad."

"What did she say?" Duncan was desperate to understand what was going on.

"Well… she said that she wasn't going out with him at all – that she wasn't going out with anyone," revealed Arthur, finally.

Duncan was silent, shocked, torn between the exhilaration of knowing that Pauline was free and the pain of the realisation that his best friend had lied to him, deceived him. Len knew how Duncan felt about Pauline and yet he had deliberately set out to stop any chance of a relationship between the two by lying. An honour code between friends had been transgressed. Duncan was angry but his rational mind warned him to avoid conflict with Len. More important – more important by far – was that he could now go and ask Pauline for a date.

They say the course of true love never runs smooth, and the relationship between Duncan and Pauline had undoubtedly started off in difficult circumstances. But an easier time was to follow. A carefree, happy time that only youth can seize. Many of the older generation who had already lived through the painful years of the First World War, found that age brought with it not only experience, but also cynicism. The closing months of 1938 and the early months of 1939 were watched by the older generation with wary and fearful eyes.

For the young folk, the toil of the working week was brushed aside by the joys of Saturday nights, for this was when the church halls held their "hops". St. Mark's, St. Peter's and St. Andrew's churches provided alternating Saturday night venues for the young folk. There they would dance the foxtrot and the waltz to a beat provided by drums, sax, double bass and piano. From time to time there would be bigger dances at the Town Hall or Belle Vue, when a full band would set everyone's feet a-tapping. "Spot" prizes for lucky dancers would bring a box of chocolates or a pretty lace hankie to the pink-cheeked winners, caught in the brilliance of the searching lights. Refreshment for the tired but happy dancers came in the form of a cup of tea. The young men would be dressed in their best, having spruced themselves up in sports jackets and flannels, while the girls (having spent the afternoon with their Marcel Wave curling irons) would pat their curls into place and work as much magic as they could on their appearance. Pauline's favourite outfit was an emerald green, artificial satin dress. The colour enhanced the rich brown of her hair and brought out the aqua tints in her eyes – a legacy, maybe, from her Irish grandmother. From her slender waist, the full skirt hung deceptively straight, in tight "sun-ray" pleats – but when she danced it spun outwards, catching the light as it spread like an opening flower around her slim legs. The collar and cuffs were in creamy white lace – a subtle embellishment that she had sewed on herself to give it a touch of class. A light stroke of Evening in Paris perfume behind her ears completed the ensemble. Duncan was mesmerised. He still couldn't quite believe that she was his girl and that they were officially courting. Len O'Donnell had accepted the situation, and his subterfuge remained an unspoken topic between the two young men. But Len couldn't hide the pangs of jealousy he felt when he saw his best friend with the girl he had once hoped would be his, in one of the coveted double seats on the back row of the Arcadia cinema.

The winter passed and the days lengthened into spring, then summer, and the rumblings in Europe rose to a crescendo. The shadow of the First World War was blotted out entirely by the impending shadow of the Second. It was in those hazy, lazy days of late summer, 1939, that Duncan took Pauline for a week's holiday, to meet his beloved mother's family in Miles Green, Staffordshire.

CHAPTER FOUR

Miles Green was a small, rural mining community; its neat and tidy rows of brick houses were surrounded by the calm of the north Staffordshire countryside. The winding, tree-lined lanes were ripe for exploration – often leading to a pretty stone church or perhaps opening out onto a distant view to the north of the ruined Mow Cop castle. It was the perfect place for a holiday for the young Manchester couple – a welcome "far cry" from the city streets.

Duncan's family (on his mother's side) owned a pair of houses and assorted outbuildings on the edge of the village. On either side of the two dwellings were long passages – ginnels – that gave access to the rear of the houses. At the back was a stone-flagged yard area, divided by a low brick wall, and a kitchen garden. At the front, the houses butted directly onto the pavement, thus providing the essential access needed for one of the two houses to be used as a shop. And what a shop! Provisions, vegetables, household goods and sweets – even the coveted nylons for the girls, from time to time. It was like an Aladdin's Cave, packed full of treasures.

The fifty or so mile journey from Manchester to Miles Green was a lengthy one, requiring several changes of transport: first the tram to Stockport town centre, then the North Western bus service to Newcastle under Lyme in the Potteries, and finally a local bus out to Miles Green. It was a hot, Saturday afternoon in late August as Duncan and Pauline trudged the final yards of their journey and were welcomed into the loving arms of their family.

"Hello duck" called Auntie Julie " ah, you're here at last. Come in, come in, Gra'mam is longing to see you".

Hugs and kisses were exchanged, the suitcases were taken from Duncan's weary grasp and the kettle was put onto the range ready for a brew. In the stifling kitchen, a tea tray was prepared and carried through to the back parlour, and the tired but happy visitors tucked into Auntie Julie's homemade fruit cake and thirstily drank the hot sweet tea.

It was such a perfect week, it seemed cruel that it should speed by so quickly.

Why is it that time seems to fly when everything is perfect and you want the hours to last for days and the days to last for years? The months ahead loomed dark and foreboding. The tender memories that would be left by those blissful days in the countryside would have to hold their sweetness for a long time to come – such carefree days would not be returning for many years.

Blissful walks in the delightful country lanes, a memorable trip to Sandbach market with Gra'mam and the best Sunday dinner that Duncan and Pauline had eaten in years. Roast beef, Yorkshire pudding, roast potatoes and fresh peas from the garden – all washed down with a cup of Tizer or better still, Auntie Julie's home made herb beer which was utterly delicious. Duncan was sure that it contained nettles, dandelions and yarrow and there were undoubtedly other things too, but when he asked about the ingredients he was told that they were secret. The entire concoction had been decanted into a dark green bottle and sealed with a cork plug, making it appear all the more mysterious. Its enigmatic charm added to the enchantment of the holiday.

But there were shadows. As darkness fell and the family drew together to chat for a while in the evening, the talk turned to Europe. Duncan and Pauline had seen the Pathe and Movietone newsreels in the Manchester cinemas and they explained to the others the worrying nature of what they'd seen – the bomb damage in Spain, the Hitler Youth in Germany and the build-up of *Nazi* power in Europe. On the Friday, while Duncan and Pauline were at Miles Green, fifty six German divisions crossed Poland's frontiers from East Prussia, Pomerania, Silesia and Slovakia, piercing the thinly spread defences. In Britain, there was unease and uncertainty. There was nervousness and fear.

Amid the gloom, the joy of the young couple's annual holiday drew to a close. They were due to return home on the Sunday, and so decided to take one last, meandering walk down the country lanes before starting the long journey back to Manchester. It was a glorious sunny morning – the sky was an azure blue and there was hardly a cloud in sight. The hedgerows bordering the narrow lanes were resplendent with late summer dog roses and honeysuckle. Here and there, a hawthorn bush was laden with blood red berries, ready for the coming winter. The walk back to the house took Pauline and Duncan through the centre of the village and past the Working Men's Club – a popular meeting place in the socialist dominated mining villages. The doors were wide open as it was a hot day and from inside the stuffy, smoky interior the voice of the Prime Minister, Neville Chamberlain, could be faintly heard coming from the crackling wireless set.

"I am speaking to you from the Cabinet Room at 10 Downing Street. This morning the British Ambassador in Berlin handed the German Government a final note stating that unless we heard from them by 11 o'clock that they were prepared at once to withdraw their troops from Poland, a state of war would exist between us. I have to tell you now, that no such undertaking has been received, and that consequently this country is at war with Germany".

There was a stunned silence in the clubhouse as Chamberlain's distinctive voice droned on. Then men inside began to stir, getting up from their seats, desperate to get back to their homes and families and break the terrible news.

"Now may God bless you all and may He defend the right," continued Chamberlain, as Duncan's cousin Georgie ran outside, eager to return home as quickly as possible. Duncan called his name and Georgie span around, breathless.

"Did you hear it? Did you hear Chamberlain's broadcast? We're at war," he gasped.

More men were spilling out of the club now, worried expressions written across their faces. Voices were raised, the air was heavy with dread. Over the road a woman leaned out of a half open sash window and cried hysterically:

"It's war, we're at war. We're all going to die".

Duncan grasped Pauline's hand tightly and protectively drew her nearer to him. People were everywhere now and the fear was palpable. The warm September morning suddenly seemed oppressively clammy; the blue sky turned threatening as nervous glances upward seemed to see shadows of enemy planes already overhead.

It was one of those unique times. One of those life-stopping times, when a universal, collective memory is shared by millions. "Where were you when it happened?" can be answered in a heartbeat, because no-one ever forgets. Remember how it was when the planes flew into the Twin Towers in New York? You know exactly where you were at that instant. You can remember every second as if it happened only moments ago. That's how it was that September Sunday in 1939. Forever etched in the memory of nations and scorched deep onto the Wall of Time.

Back at Auntie Julie's everyone had gathered and apprehension hung heavy in the air. A hasty meal was prepared for the visitors who were desperate to get back to Manchester as soon as possible, as everyone seemed to think that hostilities would start right away. Maybe the public transport system would close down too – they had to get back home as soon as they could. Though the itinerary was already planned, it was felt that now the country was at war, the bus service might be unpredictable, and who could tell how long the journey might take. Clothes were hastily stuffed into suitcases, and after many heart-rending hugs, they took their leave of the family. The streets were still full of people and a number of young lads were racing by playing at aeroplanes. The wait at the bus stop in Miles Green seemed to take forever but it was nothing compared to the wait in Newcastle under Lyme. The bus depot was full of people and a sense of panic had started to infiltrate a few faint hearts. Everyone was talking; strangers were comforting strangers. Suddenly the ominous whine of an air raid siren started up, causing mild panic and confusion amongst the waiting passengers. Eyes turned to the skies searching for the enemy – but there was nothing to be seen in the darkening blueness. The whine began to waver and then to undulate up and down.

"It's the All Clear," shouted a relieved voice in the crowd.

There was nervous laughter and a few giggles. The clamour died down and people waited patiently once more. Many weary hours later the Stockport bus arrived and the passengers gratefully clambered aboard.

As the bus made its way north towards Manchester, there were many similar journeys being taken that night – the first night of the Second World War. And many a wise soul looked around at the faces they could see – some familiar, some unknown – and wondered who amongst them would see many more Septembers, and who amongst them would perish.

CHAPTER FIVE

The strange thing was – life went on more or less the same at first. Thankfully, the swarm of enemy bombers that everyone expected to arrive immediately did not appear overnight. No bombs, no gas attacks, no marauding hordes in the streets. Nothing seemed very different – for just a little while at least – though food rationing meant that belts could be pulled in with some ease. A census (the National Register) had been compiled in late September 1939, and was used as the basis for issuing ration books and identity cards.

Preparations for defence were at the front of everyone's minds. At school, little children learned how to don their brightly coloured Mickey Mouse gas masks before they started their ABC, and Anderson air-raid shelters became *de-rigeur* for those with a yard or a bit of garden, while for those without the luxury of a patch of land, the Morrison "Table" shelters became sought after furniture. In essence, the Morrison was a rectangular steel frame construction that masqueraded as a dining table. A pretty tablecloth cleverly turned it from a portent of doom into a utilitarian piece of furniture. The blackouts themselves – aimed to make inhabited areas appear as pools of darkness to enemy aircraft – caused a wave of casualties from traffic accidents and the like. As the "Phoney War" dragged on, civil defence preparations advanced and the evacuation of thousands of Manchester school boys and girls was organised. Mothers agonised over the real possibility of having to send their beloved children away to the countryside – a heart-rending dilemma. They were torn between wanting to keep their children by their side (yet knowing the danger this could place them in) and wanting their little ones to be sent to the safety of the rural areas (yet knowing that such a parting would break the hearts of both mother and child). By the end of the year more than three hundred thousand British children had left their urban homes for safe reception areas in the countryside.

Although war wasn't the ideal means to achieve his ambition to fly, Duncan patriotically wanted to join the Royal Air Force. To his intense disappointment, however, his term of indenture with Manchester City Corporation precluded him from doing so. He had signed up as an apprentice joiner for seven years in 1935 and thus was tied until June 1942, when he would be almost twenty one. Furthermore, he was in a Reserved Occupation. His work was considered essential, for all the joiners were involved in urgent civil defence work in Manchester city centre; fitting asbestos lined, steel doors where needed, strengthening key buildings, bomb-proofing warehouses and converting cellars to air-raid bunkers. The city had a long legacy of textile manufacturing – King Cotton ruled in Manchester – and many of the old Victorian buildings in the heart of the city were fire hazards, packed to the rafters with flammable fabrics. Furthermore, the city was a major industrial port, linked by the Manchester Ship Canal to the Irish Sea. There was no doubt in anyone's minds that Manchester would be a prime target for the enemy.

At strategic locations around the city, anti-aircraft gun defences, searchlight batteries and barrage balloon operations were all set up. Manchester would be ready, but not willing. The civil defence preparations work would soon be put to the test.

In the summer of 1940, enemy bombers intent on annihilating the oil refineries at Thames Haven drifted off course and dropped their loads on central London. The "Phoney War" was no more. An escalation of the air war immediately took place on both sides and "The Few" of RAF Fighter Command defended their homeland against the threat of occupation. Retaliatory attacks were ordered against Berlin, and the Germans responded by launching further raids on London and Liverpool. The *Blitz* had begun.

Almost a year to the day after that sunny Sunday back in September 1939, a massive daylight bombing raid smashed the East End of London. Night bombing then took over as the *Luftwaffe* bombs rained down on the capital, night after night. Most raids were carried out by around one hundred and fifty bomber aircraft, but on some terrible nights over three hundred blackened the skies over London. A few weeks later in early November, Coventry city centre was all but wiped off the map in a devastating deluge of concentrated bombing brought by four hundred and forty nine enemy aircraft. Sporadic attacks followed; Birmingham, Manchester, Southampton, Sheffield, Hull, Glasgow and more. Through the autumn of 1940, Manchester had been attacked by incendiaries and oil bombs, and the civil defence and fire fighting teams had worked hard. Yet it did not fully prepare them for what was to come.

Winter crept in and Christmas was on its way. Prayers and celebrations would take place just as in any other year. The war would not stop Christmas. And so, on the Sunday evening just three days before Christmas Day, the 6.o'clock evening church services were being held throughout the city. As the congregations filled their lungs and sang their praises, or gently lulled the words of "Silent Night", the first jarring wails of the air-raid sirens disturbed the night. It had begun. The sirens would continue to wail for a full twelve hours, until the first pale rays of dawn chased away the winged enemy.

The bombs rained down on a city that had only a depleted fire-fighting force in place – for many of the Manchester firemen had been called out to help nearby Liverpool which had been heavily attacked two nights previously. Volunteers and reserve fire fighters were called in from all surrounding areas, and as the Manchester firemen hastily returned to their home town, their hearts were heavy when they saw the luminous, blood red glow over their city centre. It was a long and terrible night. Searchlights combed the skies hunting for the *Luftwaffe* aircraft. Anti-aircraft guns rattled out into the night. One of them jammed, its return switch malfunctioning. The frantic gunner rammed home the ammunition with his bare hands, catching his flesh in the breech mechanism as he made the gun ready to fire. For eleven more hours he would ram home the heavy ammunition with bleeding and bruised fingers. It was his duty. Morning saw the exhausted firemen desperately trying to damp down the city fires. Glowing embers would be a beacon to draw bombers to the area when night fell again. And sure enough, they did. Another night of non-stop, concentrated bombing hit the city.

A group of young women setting off for the 7.30pm night shift to make parachutes, heard the sirens begin to wail. As the first incendiaries began to fall around them, they took shelter under a staircase in the city centre factory. The bombs continued throughout the night yet again, testing the overworked and totally exhausted fire crews to the limit. When silence fell, the women emerged on Christmas Eve as dawn broke and looked with horror at the scene around them. Debris, jagged shards of glass, broken buildings and above all, a pervading and acrid smell of burning. Walking down Oxford Street toward the shattered remains of what was once the proud and splendid Manchester Free Trade Hall, they saw the fire engines and the weary crews battling to damp the final flames. One of the women straggled a little, gazing at the smashed remnants of an expensive fashion shop that she had often stared into and dreamed the dreams of the poor. There, on the pavement in front of the shop, lay several fur coats and luscious, thick mink stoles, blasted out from the window display when the glass had shattered into thousands of tiny pieces. The shards glistened like diamonds in the rosy dawn light. She looked at the furs and shrugged her shoulders. With a wistful expression on her smoke grimed face she walked on, picking her way carefully around the furs. Looters would be shot.

Homes, factories, shops. Churches, theatres, schools. Hospitals, public buildings and hotels. Many people had been killed, thousands had been made homeless. Few escaped the Manchester *Blitz*. An unlucky thirteen aircraft under construction at the Metro Vickers factory had been obliterated by the attacks – they were the first of the new Avro Manchester bombers and had been eagerly awaited by the RAF. Against all the odds, however, the following day, hot pies, puddings and custard were provided for all those who had been bombed out of their homes. It was still Christmas.

And when it seemed it would never stop, it finally did. In the spring of 1941 the bombers were re-deployed to Eastern Europe.

CHAPTER SIX

The bomb damage in Manchester was indescribable. Unforgettable. Heart rending. Duncan spent his days working on the damaged buildings and the sights he saw made him determined to try yet again to join the RAF. This time his hopes were raised and he was called for assessment. The interview at Dover Street in Manchester was tough and there was a battery of tests that had to be passed before he could be considered for air crew. The intelligence tests were not too hard, and Duncan's recent Building College training in subjects like geometry and geography had certainly helped. The physical tests were challenging for the nineteen year old, and some were predetermined by factors such as eyesight, but Duncan's excellent 20/20 vision and strong physique got him through. He was a keen swimmer, and physically very active, plus a thousand and one rides on his old Hercules bike had helped to strengthen his already sturdy, young frame. The doctor had handed him a tube of mercury with the instruction to blow into it for one entire minute so as to test his lung strength. Duncan exhaled until he felt his ribcage would implode. As he blew, his memories took him back to the day when he had huffed and puffed, carrying his brand new bike up the stairs to show to his mother, as she lay in her sick bed. It seemed an eternity ago. It was.

The physical tests seemed straightforward, and Duncan knew right away that he had passed them. More of a challenge was the aptitude test to see if he had the mind-set to handle Morse Code. The training rooms at Manchester's College of Science and Technology on Whitworth Street were fully equipped with the kit needed for these tests, and as Duncan sat at the bench in the examination room, his palms were moist with nervousness. He badly wanted to pass the test – pilots and specifically, wireless operators, needed to use Morse. He was handed a pair of rubber earphones and he carefully put them on with an apparent confidence that he didn't entirely possess. The earphones felt uncomfortably strange and they masked the noises in the room to a dull muffle. A tape recorder was started and Duncan carefully listened to the unfamiliar staccato sounds, as two lots of Morse Code were fed in over the earphones. His task was to match the pairs and pick out the dissimilar ones. The idea was to see if the applicant could differentiate between different Morse sounds. If they all sounded the same to him it would be unlikely that he could ever learn to understand and broadcast Morse Code, and the chance of becoming a pilot or wireless operator would no longer be an option open to him. Concentrating and listening hard to match the tones and pick out differences in sound length, Duncan ticked the exam sheet in what he felt were the correct places. The hour-long test seemed to go on forever but finally he was able to peel off the hot earphones and relax for a few moments. He looked around at the other candidates sitting the test. From the corner of his eye he had seen several of them "weeded out" as the test had progressed. He was still there, so the examiners must have thought that he was in with a chance. It would surely be only a few days before the results would be through, but Duncan could hardly bear to wait. He wanted to defend his country, to fight for his country, to fly for his country. His childhood dream – a chance to fly – was about to become reality in a way that he could never have envisaged a decade or so earlier.

The direction of the war had changed – heavy bombers were needed and there was much pressure to increase the recruitment of air crew. Just a few days after the tests, Duncan received an envelope marked O.H.M.S.

"On His Majesty's Service" he whispered as his fingers tore at the envelope. "Please let me pass, please" he silently prayed.

He read the words but couldn't believe them at first. He read them again. He was in. Relief washed over him. His application had got the green light – he'd been accepted into the RAF Volunteer Reserve. The position of Wireless Operator-Air Gunner (WOp/AG) was offered, but there was much to be done before Duncan could get his wings. The letter explained that in the months to come, before he would receive his official call-up, he must undergo preparatory training in Manchester, to learn Morse Code, navigation, aircraft recognition and RAF protocol. Pauline greeted his news with a mixture of pride and fear, but the awful moment of parting wasn't yet upon them. In fact it would be almost a year before he would leave. And it would be a very busy year.

To today's younger generations familiar with mobile phones and sophisticated computer networks, Morse Code must seem an archaic method of communication. Back in the early 1940s, however, it was an invaluable means of transmitting vital information between aircraft and their command bases. Amazingly, it had been invented in the mid 1800s – when Samuel Finley Breese Morse (a one-time artist from Massachusetts) had first lodged the patent for his novel telegraphic method that included an innovative dot and dash code. Within a few years of its creation, Morse Code, as a system of electronic communication, was in international use.

Learning it was a challenge. For two evenings each week Duncan joined his fellow RAF Volunteer Reservists at the College of Science and Technology on Whitworth Street where he had previously taken his aptitude test. For some, learning Morse would prove to be an impossible task; for others, it became a gradually acquired skill. The aim, for a good operator, was to arrive at an almost thought-free process of recognition. Through constant practice (parrot fashion), reading and transmitting the code slowly became more familiar and eventually even second nature to many of the young lads; almost a reflex action in fact.

In Morse code, the letters of the alphabet are represented by dots and dashes, and are heard or spoken as dit (for the dot) and dah (for the dash). Common letters such as *E* and *A* were quick and easily recognizable. The letter *E* was shown as a single dot and heard as the sound dit. The letter *A* was shown as a dot dash, or dit dah. A less often used letter such as X had the more complex representation of dit dah dah dit, and could be written out as ._ _ . Between these sounds were graduated intervals of silence, the differing length of pause indicating another letter, or a new word. The best operators learned the sound of the character and knew that, above all, if one letter was not recognised, it was imperative to miss it out and carry on. Time wasted decoding an individual sound would mean that other letters would be missed and the gist of the entire message lost.

Within the first few hours, most trainees managed to read a few four letter words at a speed of five words per minute. When the ten word per minute barrier was met, the trainee felt he was on the way to competency. By the end of the course, Duncan had managed to achieve the level that was needed to be a Wireless Operator – eighteen words a minute – and so he took a step closer to the war. The months passed quickly. In June 1942, just a few weeks before his twenty first birthday, Duncan received his formal "call up" into the RAF. He was posted to Padgate just outside Manchester and spent three days being kitted out. His life would never be the same again.

CHAPTER SEVEN

The Manchester train moved slowly along the tracks as it finally pulled into Blackpool's Central Station. It had seemed a long journey from Manchester's Exchange Station – across the flat mosses and then the green fields of the Lancashire Fylde. It was almost midsummer, and it was uncomfortably hot in the carriage. Duncan had looked out at the countryside, but his thoughts were back home in Manchester with Pauline, for his heart was still aching at their recent emotional parting.

His mind went back a few months to the day they had got engaged. The stones in her ring had caught the light as she had turned it this way and that. He had looked at her sweet face and noticed a tear slowly sliding down her cheek. It had lain there, glistening for a moment before she had quickly wiped it away, hoping that he hadn't noticed. Duncan had found a little jeweller's shop – Woods on Stretford Road in Hulme – while he was working on bomb damaged homes in the area. Knowing that he would be receiving his call-up any day, he had been determined to buy an engagement ring for her. He knew it would make him feel just a little more comfortable if she was his fiancée, when the dreaded moment of parting eventually arrived. He had very little money, but he had secretly been saving all he possibly could to buy her the ring. When he kissed her goodbye at the station, she had had tears in her eyes again. She waved to him as the train made its lumbering, rhythmic way along the tracks, and the ring glittered in the sunlight as her hand had slowly, reluctantly, bade him farewell.

Wearily, Duncan lifted his bulging kit bag down from the luggage rack. Leaning out through the open carriage window he tugged hard at the handle and the door sprang open. The station concourse at Blackpool was packed with people, just as it had been ten months earlier when a twin engined Blackburn Botha aircraft had crashed down onto the station after a freak mid air collision with another training aircraft in the cloudy skies over the holiday town. It had been an unseasonably cool Thursday in late August and the station had been packed with holidaymakers enjoying a break away from thoughts of war. The Botha (an inefficient, rejected torpedo bomber, relegated to a training rôle) had crashed through the roof of the entrance hall of the Central Station, showering burning aviation fuel over the crowds who were buying tickets and waiting to board trains. A massive conflagration had followed and a huge cloud of thick black smoke had risen several hundred feet over the centre of the town. Holidaymakers on the beach and the promenade had been shocked at the sight of the plane as it made its spiral dive to the ground – the massive plume of smoke bearing witness to its final demise. Eighteen people lost their lives in the catastrophe, many of them incarcerated amongst the tangled ironwork and debris. One family had come to Blackpool from London, under a wartime rest scheme. By an ironical curse of ill fortune they had escaped the London *Blitz* only to meet their untimely deaths in the popular holiday resort of Blackpool. It could have been worse. Had the London train not pulled out of the station just a few minutes earlier, the toll would have been far greater.

The roof of Central Station had been rebuilt by the time Duncan arrived there in the early summer of 1942. To the casual observer, there was little sign of the earlier tragedy. Blackpool was at heart, a holiday town, and even war couldn't dampen its spirits. The Golden Mile that ran from the North Pier near Bispham to the Pleasure Beach at the southern end of the town, was the draw for everyone. It seemed almost incongruous that this happy holiday town should also be the home to many thousands of trainee servicemen and women. The airfield at Squire's Gate had been acquired by the military in the early days of the war, and Blackpool's famous Winter Gardens was the venue for the initial training of many RAF air crew. A melting pot of evacuees, displaced civil servants, holiday makers and airmen were all made welcome in Blackpool. The trainee servicemen were given a special Forces admission price of 6d to all the places of entertainment owned by the Blackpool Tower and Winter Gardens Company. The white flashes on their caps indicated they were trainee air crew, and it gave pleasure to many a young lad to discover that it would also earn him a free drink as well as a grateful smile.

Like most of the other lads, Duncan was billeted in civilian digs. Some of his pals struck lucky. Not so Duncan! Bedbugs and barely edible food were all he had to look forward to at the end of each day. Route marched from their digs in the morning (in Duncan's case he was glad to be leaving) the trainees spent their days studying, marching and training on the firing range and more. Except for Wednesday afternoons. That was for sports. What a delight it was to march to Stanley Park or Derby Baths and forget for a while that soon there was a war to be fought.

The weekends were free time, and many lads were happy to stay and enjoy the delights of Blackpool and its Pleasure Beach. Not so Duncan! His one desire was to get back to Manchester to see Pauline. He walked along the promenade to Bispham and took up his position at the roadside, hoping that his distinctive Air Force blue uniform would help him get a lift. It wasn't too long before he spotted a promising lorry. The driver pulled up alongside and pushing his dusty cap to the back of his head, called out,

"Where are you heading, air man?"

Duncan explained that he needed to get to Manchester and the driver beamed his encouragement.

"Got a girl there, have you? You're in luck, I'm on my way there. Hop in the back, lad."

Duncan's relief that he had found a lift so quickly was soon overtaken by the realisation that his salvation was actually a lorry from Jackson's Brick Works that had just dumped its load at the nearby Squire's Gate airport and was now on its way back to Longsight for more bricks. The back of the open lorry was full of reddish brown brick dust that swirled around, getting into his hair and eyes as the engine roared into life and the vehicle gathered speed. Duncan tried to get into the area that was sheltered by the driver's cab, but the ruddy dust swirled remorselessly around him. He resigned himself to the situation and concentrated on the delightful knowledge that he would soon be seeing Pauline. As he sat, smiling to himself, he felt the first heavy rain drops fall ominously onto the back of his hand. Within moments the heavens opened and the rain became a deluge, changing the brick dust into thick, dark red slurry that stained Duncan's Air Force blue an undesirable maroon. He gathered his waterproof ground sheet (that doubled up as a cape) around his upper body, trying to protect his jacket from the slurry, but nothing could keep the red mess off the lower part of his trousers. When the lorry finally came to a stop in Manchester, Duncan emerged a sorry sight. The driver looked at him ruefully and wished him well, as Duncan trudged away to his father's house. It was going to take some cleaning and brushing to smarten up his best blues in time for his return the following day – Duncan prayed that his father and Ida would help him rather than hinder him (though he knew the latter was most likely).

There were other weekend trips back to Manchester to see Pauline over the ensuing weeks of Duncan's RAF training at

Blackpool. The journey there was always full of happiness and anticipation – the journey back was drenched in sadness and longing. Whilst together they would treasure every moment, and talk about their plans to get married the following year, when they had managed to save up some money. Dreaming of a happy future, an idyllic time where there would be no war and no fighting, helped them to live through their weeks apart.

One hot August Saturday, however, when Duncan discovered the machinations wrought by his father, things changed. As he rushed to meet Pauline and their eyes locked, he realised that all was not well. She seemed angry and distressed, her eyes brimming with tears. She could hardly contain herself as she gasped out:

"Duncan, an awful thing has happened. I met your brother Ken yesterday and he was wearing a smart new suit. I've never seen him looking so well dressed and so I remarked on it to him. I couldn't believe what he said. I was so angry I was shaking. He told me that your father had bought it for him out of your money. YOUR money."

She gulped for air and sobbed at the same time. Her anger was palpable. Duncan stared at her as the enormity of what she was saying sank in.

"Your money. Our money. The money we're saving so we can get married. He bought your brother Ken a suit with **our** wedding money."

Pauline was trembling with anger, but it was nothing to the fury that welled up inside Duncan. His father had taken, **no** – had stolen – had squandered, Duncan's rightful money. The money that was being paid by his employer, Manchester Corporation, while he was in service. The money that he believed his father was putting in the bank for him so that he could marry Pauline one day soon. It was a substantial amount, over three pounds a week, while Duncan was getting by with the fourteen shillings that the Air Force was paying him. He determined to confront his father right away.

Outwardly calm, yet inwardly raging, Duncan's knuckles beat a tattoo on the back door of the familiar terraced house that he had once called "home". Ida answered the door and casually beckoned him in. She never looked pleased to see him and the feeling was entirely mutual, as Duncan found her presence provoked a nasty taste in his mouth. He entered the little scullery and nodded an acknowledgement to both his father and grandfather, who were seated either side of the empty fire grate. John, his paternal grandfather, nodded back while his father, Eddie, smiled a welcome that was loaded with false *bonhomie*. The presence of both his father and grandfather was daunting – Duncan could still feel the stinging pain of many cuffs and knocks that he'd taken from Eddie's rough and calloused hands over the years. He swallowed hard and took a deep breath.

"Dad, my money, the three pounds that the Corporation pays me every week, you said you would save it up for Pauline and me – what's happened to it? Have you spent it? Our Ken told Pauline that you bought him a new suit with it – why? How could you do that – I don't understand – why?"

Bewildered and perplexed by the apparent treachery wrought by his father, Duncan could still not believe his own flesh and blood would betray his trust in such a callous fashion. He had to hear it from his father's lips before he could accept it to be true. But no such admission was forthcoming from Eddie. Glib, false and as slippery as a snake, Eddie avoided the direct question by telling his eldest son that a big and sumptuous wedding would be planned for him. He spun his shallow flattery and charm, avoiding any mention of how his son's money was being spent, but it was clear that Duncan didn't believe a word of it. When

Eddie realized his ruse wasn't working, he fell back on to his old ways and raised his hand as if to strike his son. Though he felt intimidated, Duncan stood his ground. Taller and stronger now than his father – Eddie wouldn't be able to make him suffer as he had when Duncan was a little boy. The bruises and red welts from cruel beatings lived on in his memory. There would be no more. He faced his father and in a calm voice that belied his emotional state of mind he said:

"I'll collect my things and go. I think that would be best."

There wasn't much to collect and no one made an attempt to stop him. Leaving the house that had been his home for many years was not easy. Though the recent times had been soul-less and empty, the early days when his beloved mother was alive had been happy ones. He recalled her tender touch and her sad words. His eyes saw only her lovely face, until his tears washed the precious vision away. He walked out vowing never to set foot in the house again.

CHAPTER EIGHT

"Do you take this woman to be your lawful wedded wife?"
"I do".
The words rang strong and true around the walls in Manchester's All Saints Registry Office. He looked at her and his heart almost burst with love. Standing beside him, clad in a flattering, fitted suit, carrying a bouquet of flowers, she seemed to him like a perfect angel. He knew she had wanted a white wedding in church, but they had neither the money nor the time. She looked at him, in his Air Force blue uniform and she filled with pride and love. The money he'd planned on saving for their wedding was gone, squandered by Eddie. They were left with nothing. But at least now that she was his wife, the three pounds a week would go straight to her and not Eddie. No more free suits for Ken, no more beer and cigarette money for Eddie. They were free. They were together. Together until the war would take him away again. And now they had a week together. One entire precious week for their honeymoon.

Pauline had spent the past two days in a hectic whirl organising the wedding. Nothing could be firmed up or planned with certainty until Duncan had passed out at Blackpool, because no leave was granted until the trainee airmen had got through their final exams. Early in October Duncan had telephoned her to break the good news that he had passed – forty eight hours later they were married.

The guests were just a few of Pauline's family and some close friends of both the bride and groom. No one from Duncan's family was invited, nor indeed would they have attended. The wedding was scheduled for nine a.m., on October 9th and so

Pauline had risen early. It was her wedding day – the most special and important day in a woman's life, so they say.

"Get the coal in Pauline and light a fire in the grate" her mother called. "We need to warm the house before the visitors come round after your wedding".

Pauline scurried to do as she was bid. She was exhausted, having spent the previous day getting everything ready, including baking an *ersatz* chocolate cake, with all its *faux* ingredients, the best that rationing could do to produce a wedding cake for her. She set the table and dusted the front room again, finding it hard to believe that her mother and sister didn't seem to want to lift a finger to help her. She knew they felt some resentment towards the marriage, yet she couldn't understand what it was. Her sister was surely just jealous – that was nothing new, she had always been jealous of Pauline. Not that it was Pauline's fault that Ethel was neither as pretty nor as charming as her elder sister. And jealousy was never a flattering garment to wear. Her brother, Joe, was the only one who helped. Glancing at his watch he shooed Pauline away from the chores and insisted she put the finishing touches to her outfit in time to leave the house.

And so now they were married. Husband and wife. Seven days of wedded bliss were theirs – and where was the honeymoon to be? Where else but Miles Green, where they were always welcome and felt so safe and happy? A place full of good memories – a place that would harbour more. But happy days pass so quickly, while dreaded, lonely, sad days drag. The one short week went by like a dream; but with each passing day came the certain knowledge that they would soon be parting. After seven days, his young bride was left alone as Duncan returned to the Air Force to undertake Advanced Wireless Training at Madley. War called.

RAF Madley (known locally as "the drome") was situated near the village of Kingstone in Herefordshire. It was a bleak place, newly set up and not overly welcoming, and it was packed with young airmen. Known as Number 4 Radio School, Madley assumed critical importance in the early 1940s when over four thousand wireless operators (known as WOPs) were trained there. The work was hard and intensive, and the days passed slowly. The weather didn't help for it was cold and damp, with mud everywhere. November became December and soon Christmas beckoned. Rationing was making things hard for everyone, and even commonplace items like soap were now only obtainable with coupons. Ingenuity often came into play and the Ministry of Food suggested that a Christmassy sparkle could be given to holly sprigs by dipping them in a solution of Epsom salts and allowing it to dry. The officers in charge of supplies at Madley weren't bothered about adding sparkle, they simply realised that there was not enough food to feed their charges, and all trainees were sent home for Christmas. What a delight. A few precious days with his young wife in Manchester, before a long return journey to Herefordshire.

While Duncan was away, Pauline had been working in the TB offices in Manchester and carrying out Air Raid warden duties in the evening. Soon after Duncan returned to Madley, however, she too, was called up. Because she was married, her choice was to work in a war-effort factory or join the fire brigade. The very idea of climbing ladders terrified her, so she chose to work in the Fairey Aviation factory at nearby Heaton Chapel, where her secretarial experience and skills with the comptometer adding machines earned her a coveted place in the planning office. Under construction at Fairey's were the Handley Page Halifax heavy bombers. The cacophony of sound in the place made conversation hard at times, as the vast metal sheets were pounded with rivets by the airframe fitters. Pauline was tired and weary. She'd been sleeping badly in the single room she was renting – and she wasn't eating properly. She missed her husband dreadfully and she worried about him, and of course she worried about the war. What it would bring to them. What it would take away. But everyone was in the same boat. Everywhere you turned, mothers were yearning for their missing sons and daughters, wives were crying for their husbands. She had to be brave, she had to keep her fears and troubles from Duncan. He had enough on his mind, training to be a wireless operator.

At Madley, after their three month training stint, the men gathered to hear their next posting; groans and cries of jealousy rent the air as they heard others getting the choicest locations. As a northerner, Duncan's next posting to prestigious RAF Hendon, just outside London, was a cause of good-natured friction with his acquaintances from the south of England.

Hendon had status, Hendon had history. The country's first Aerial Derby had been staged there in 1912, as well as later Air Pageants and Tournaments – everyone in aviation knew Hendon. Today it is home to the famous RAF Museum; back in the 1940s it was home to Duncan and many other young airmen, for a few short months. Duncan was thrilled to know he was to be posted there, though he wisely kept his pleasure hidden so as not to irritate his pals who were destined for less illustrious places. Soon, kit bags were packed, directions and instructions were duly handed out, and many new-found friendships were dissolved as each batch of trainees moved on. Duncan's journey from Madley to Hendon was arduous. First the long and grimy ride by steam train from Hereford to Marylebone Station, then his first encounter with the unfamiliarity of London's Underground system as he took the tube to Hendon. Duncan carefully followed the printed instructions he'd been given – the locals would have known, of course, but the northern lad from Manchester was green around the gills when it came to having any sort of knowledge of the geography of Greater London. He got off the tube at Hendon Central, and asked the station guard for directions to the RAF base. The man looked at him in amusement.

"Oh crikey, you should have stayed on the tube for another stop and got off at Colindale. That's the nearest tube station to RAF Hendon. You've got a heck of a walk ahead of you now mate – it's a mile or more."

Wearily Duncan slung his kit bag over his shoulder, and, tucking his gas mask under one arm and his tin hat under the other, he set off to the next place he would call home. Number 24 Squadron, RAF Hendon.

CHAPTER NINE

Duncan climbed on board the twin engine Lockheed Hudson bomber. Painted in camouflage finish, with its matching RAF roundels on each wing, it was the first aircraft that he had ever been inside and he was fascinated by every facet of its construction. But he had to concentrate, for his task was to carry out the daily inspection of the aircraft's radio equipment as part of his training programme. It was the third day that he'd been on board the Lockheed Hudson, while it was parked just off the landing strip at Hendon, carrying out the servicing tasks. It took a bit of getting used to, because the plane was American built and its equipment was a little different to that which Duncan had become familiar with. The aircraft had seen early action in the War but by the start of 1943 it had been relegated to secondary activities such as transportation and training, its rôle here at Hendon. Parked up outside the main hangars, it was used by the trainee wireless operators to practise their vital daily servicing routines.

As Duncan sat operating the equipment, the pilot climbed aboard and nodded a greeting. Duncan turned and grinned, still a little bashful in the presence of such authority.

Casually fastening on his helmet, the pilot nodded at Duncan. "I'm just about to take the kite up, check her out," he smiled. "How would you like a spin? You can test the radio while we're up."

Duncan couldn't believe it. One minute he was sitting there, quietly going about his routine inspection, the next minute he'd been asked if he wanted to fly. Fly. To fly. He was so excited he could hardly find his voice. He cleared his throat and tried to sound casual – as if flying, taking to the air, was something that he did every day – and not the one thing that he had been dreaming of since he first saw the Barnstormers on the Highfield Road hay field in Manchester.

"Oh yes please, sir. Yes." Duncan hadn't used the right terminology, and his awe of the pilot earned the man a formal "sir" instead of the more usual "skipper." The pilot smiled to himself – this WOP was a sprog, he'd clearly never been up before, but he was a nice looking, friendly lad who seemed eager to please.

"First time up?" The pilot knew the answer before he asked the question, but he felt that a little conversation would ease things.

Duncan nodded in reply – it was hard to find his voice, he was so excited. His heart was pounding faster than he thought possible and his mouth was dry as a bone. He attempted to continue with his tasks on the radio equipment, but he was overawed at the situation he had unexpectedly found himself in. With a little help from the engineers out on the tarmac, the propellers began to rotate and the engines of the Lockheed Hudson roared into life. The pilot slowly manoeuvred the aircraft out towards the main runway; bumping and rocking a little as it traversed the uneven ground. Suddenly the speed increased and the engines began to strain.

"Prepare for take off" shouted the pilot, over the engines' roar.

Duncan was too overwhelmed to reply. Drinking in every second, committing it to memory, desperate to make a mental record of his first time in flight, all he could do was gasp. The thrust of the aircraft was amazing. The whole frame seemed to shake as it sped along the runway, building speed. Faster, faster and then suddenly they were up. Angled skyward, soaring higher and higher with every second. The ground fell away: trees, hangars, roads and surrounding buildings all seemed to shrink in size as the Lockheed Hudson made its ascent. Banking the aircraft gently as it soared even higher, the pilot called out to Duncan,

"We're at five thousand feet. Look over to the left of the aircraft and you'll be able to see the Welsh Harp reservoir."

It was a near cloudless day in late January – the sort of crisp winter's day that freezes the breath yet gladdens the soul. The last few winters had been exceptionally cold and snowy, but in contrast the past month had been mild and very wet. A brief cold front had brought a temporary respite from the drenching in southern England, and the Hertfordshire landscape was stretched out below in clear, bright relief. It was exhilarating to be up so high. The engines droned on, changing their note slightly as the plane banked again.

Duncan realised that he should attend to the radio equipment and do some testing, but it was simply impossible to drag his eyes away from the view outside the window. The pilot turned round in his seat and smiled at what he saw. He was pleased that he'd been able to take the young trainee WOP up on his first flight. Glad that he had been able to share the magic. God knows the sprog would soon be getting his fair share of the down side of it all – most of these young lads were destined for the heavy bombers. He'd get enough flying in soon enough and it wouldn't be a picnic, that's for sure. Let him enjoy this first short flight.

As the Lockheed Hudson made its approach for landing there was a flurry of activity on the ground at Hendon. Passing low over the airfield, Duncan could see what appeared to be an ambulance racing along the roadway. Touchdown was only a little bumpy, for the pilot was an old hand and well used to the landing strip here. Still breathless with elation, Duncan gathered his kit together and made ready to leave the aircraft, thanking his benefactor profusely as they both exited the plane. His thanks were interrupted by the strident ringing of a Red Cross ambulance. An engineer ran up to the two airmen, calling out,

"You've missed a nasty accident. Happened just a few minutes ago. An erk – one of the ground crew, he ... he..." His voice faltered as he gestured toward a cluster of people in the distance, grouped around a de Havilland Dominie bi-plane. The ambulance stood alongside.

"What's gone on?" asked the pilot.

"One of the new erks just bought it. The Dominie had already started up and the bloke just walked right into one of the propellers. He didn't stand a chance. It was a hell of a mess. They'll be scraping bits of him off the fuselage for weeks I reckon. His friend was sick on the spot. I can tell you I wasn't far off that too. Hell of a mess." The man shook his head, slowly, his face pale and sweaty with shock.

The grisly news stunned Duncan. It came in such sharp contrast to the exhilarating experience he'd just had, soaring high above the airfield. It was hard to take in the fact that in those same few moments, a young man had been cut to pieces by an aircraft propeller. Life was cruel. Death was far crueler.

CHAPTER TEN

Throughout the long months of 1940 the RAF had suffered tragic, heavy losses. Daytime bombing had resulted in the decimation of many allied aircraft. They were easy targets – sitting ducks – and so in 1941 the night offensive had begun, in the hope that the planes would not be seen so easily under cover of darkness.

Winston Churchill had addressed the country:

"The Navy can lose us the war, but only the Air Force can win it. Therefore our supreme effort must be to gain overwhelming mastery in the air. The Fighters are our salvation, but the Bombers alone provide the means of victory."

The appointment (in early 1942) of Sir Arthur "Bomber" Harris as head of Bomber Command marked the change in direction. A quiet man, he was not easy to know, or indeed, understand – he was, however, imbued with great personal commitment and formidable strength of character. Dynamic and driven, Harris believed that air power, through strategic bombing, was the way to win the war and bring a return to peace. New and better aircraft in the shape of the mighty Lancaster would change the scene. Navigational aids and technical advances plus various crucial, strategic innovations and tactics paved the way forward. A massive air crew training programme was put into operation – and Duncan was part of it. The young airmen would need everything they learned and more. Flying in a bomber was possibly the most dangerous job imaginable. Around fifty five thousand air crew would die in raids over Europe between 1939 and 1945 – the highest loss rate of any major branch of the British armed forces. Though the trainees knew they were in for a hard time, few of them let it enter their consciousness. They were young volunteers – most were in their early twenties – they were brave and they were going to fight for their country. "Youth is ever proud to visit the margins of death".

Training air crew was a lengthy business. It took around twelve months for a pilot to learn to fly a heavy bomber and around the same length of time to teach a navigator all he needed to know. The flight engineer's training was shorter, usually around six months, for many of them were already motor mechanics in civilian life and their vocation had readied them for their new rôle. Quickest by far was the air gunnery training – just a twelve week stretch prepared them for their front-line task. At the other end of the scale was the wireless operator. Before the war began, a wireless operator's training had taken two full years, but air crew were needed desperately and the WOP's training was cut to around eighteen months intensive work before he could gain his sergeant's stripes and see the real action. There was a vast amount of technical detail to absorb, including the obvious on-board training as well as experience at the "home" end of radio operations too. For the novice wireless operators there was also gunnery training, as bomber crews were expected to take on the rôles of other crew members in an emergency, and it was the WOP's task to fill in if a gunner was injured or killed. By the later stages of the war the WOP's training had been condensed to just six months – so great was the need to fill the shoes of those poor souls who never returned.

In the late spring of 1943, Duncan was moved back to RAF Madley for flying training. He was sorry to leave Hendon. As he slowly packed his kit bag he remembered the happier days that had contrasted with the horror stories that had frequently filtered back to them. He smiled as he recalled the oranges and bananas (fruits that were scarce because of rationing) brought back from Gibraltar by 24 Squadron from RAF Transport Command who flew special sorties down to the Mediterranean with supplies and various VIPs. He remembered vividly his own first flight, and the wonder of being able to gaze down at the glinting blue waters of the Welsh Harp reservoir in gentle Hertfordshire. With some regrets, he collected his travel warrant and trudged up to Colindale tube station. As he glanced back over his shoulder at the barracks shrouded in early morning mist Duncan wondered if he would ever see Hendon again.

Crossing London via the underground, Duncan peered out of the small diamond shape in the middle of the tube train's window to check what station he was at. The train windows were covered to protect passengers from flying glass should the windows be broken by bomb blast, and it was hard to see through the grime that covered the remaining clear space. He saw the station sign "St. Pancras" looming up out of the darkness and collected his kit bag from the overhead rack. From St. Pancras he had to change to the Circle Line, and head for Paddington, his route out to Hereford and RAF Madley. Making his way across the station platforms, he noticed the signs of habitation, as many Londoners took shelter there during air raids. The posters on the walls asked "Is your journey really necessary?" "Yes" murmured Duncan to himself.

Only a few short weeks earlier a dreadful incident had happened on the underground at Bethnal Green, though it was hushed up by the authorities who hadn't wanted to spread any more alarm than was necessary. It had happened in the early evening on a rainy night, as hundreds were trying to descend into the perceived safety of the tube station so as to escape an impending air-raid. The startling sound of anti-aircraft rockets, an unfamiliar device only recently introduced into the air defences, panicked the crowd who then pushed forward down the stairs. At the bottom, a young woman with a baby in her arms tripped and fell. More, then more, fell onto her and onto each other, crushing and crushing. One hundred and seventy three died in their vain attempt to reach safety.

Other hazards of sheltering in the tube, though less deadly, were certainly unpleasant. Plagues of mosquitoes descended on the warm bodies and lice frequently crawled from head to head. In the early days of the *blitz* there were few hygienic arrangements and people would walk into the tunnels to relieve themselves. The resultant stench was understandably overwhelming, and so facilities were set up to improve the temporary living conditions. Stench or no stench, it was better than staying above ground when the bombs were dropping.

Duncan's journey was long and tiring and the sight of the RAF transport van waiting at Hereford railway station was the best welcome he could have wished for. A weak smile and nodded thanks to the driver earned him a friendly greeting and soon they were leaving the pretty town, crossing the meandering River Wye and heading southwest on the A 465 towards Madley. He glanced back at the soaring spires of Hereford Cathedral catching the last golden rays of the sun, and thought how peaceful it was.

In contrast, Madley was a hive of activity. Much had happened since Duncan was last there in December. Concrete and tarmac replaced the muddy tracks and solid billets replaced the ramshackle and damp constructions that had been there the previous winter. The aerodrome was situated in the flat, wide floodplain of the River Wye to the east of the Golden Valley, and the views over toward the Black Mountains of Wales were breathtaking in the morning sun. But there was no time to admire the view. Flying training on board de Havilland Dominies and Percival Proctor aircraft was immediately begun for the trainees. Duncan had been pleased to spot some familiar faces amongst the lads, in particular a fellow from Beeston called Eric Antony, who he'd trained with at Blackpool. Eric was a decent sort, a happy-go-lucky lad who had lived with his sister since their parents had died. The two young airmen swapped stories of their recent training courses whilst waiting to be assigned to their first official flight. They boarded a twin engined Dominie bi-plane along with four other wireless operator trainees and settled into the cramped space, ready for take off.

The Dominie was a small military aircraft, a "sister" to the de Havilland Rapide that had seen happier times taking passengers from London to Paris. As the aircraft stood only ten feet or so in height it was easy to climb on board her and she was a trustworthy flying classroom. For most of the trainees it was their very first flight, though some (like Duncan) had been in the air before. The excitement was palpable as they taxied down the runway and took off, climbing rapidly at around 150 miles an hour, leaving the green fields and hedgerows of Herefordshire far below. The novice WOPs took it in turns to operate the wireless transmitter receivers, calling back to base and alternately looking out of the windows at the patchwork of fields and villages a thousand feet or more below them. The flight was as smooth as butter until their course took them over the Black Mountains, part of the Brecon Beacon range. As the little aircraft climbed, the turbulence began. At first it was just like travelling over a rough and un-made road, but then they hit an air pocket and the Dominie dropped a hundred feet or so. The trainees grinned and hung on to their seats, no-one wanted to appear nervous or less brave than his fellows. The pilot thoughtfully cut short their time over the mountains.

"Best not to make you all air sick on your first time up" he shouted to his young passengers, assured of their gratitude by the chorus of assent.

Not every pilot was so considerate. After the docile Dominies, the young trainees were sent up on single engined, dual seater Percival Proctors. Most of the pilots who took them up were fighter pilots who had just completed their "tour" of thirty operations. They were the lucky ones who had survived against the odds and were now waiting for their transfer to other types of aircraft, and in the meantime they were helping to train the young WOPs. It must have seemed so tame, so quiet and safe after their experiences in the terror-ridden skies over mainland Europe. Perhaps in an effort to prepare the trainees for what was soon to come, most of the pilots put their aircraft through a series of gentle acrobatics, or as they euphemistically termed it "throwing the kite around".

Sergeant Matejale was one such "gung-ho" pilot. He and his Polish colleagues had undergone extreme hardship and exceptionally dangerous conditions in their journey to Britain to fight (as Matajele termed them) the *Bosche*. Determined to make his charges appreciate the dangers of what they would soon be facing, he would bank the little aircraft sharply and perform what seemed to be crazed manoeuvres, which usually resulted in the WOPs being airsick. When it happened to Duncan, on his first time up with Matajele, his head spun as the aircraft plummeted and then rose again, banked and dived. The nausea was overwhelming and uncontrollable – it was also mortifying. Even more so when Duncan was made to clean the mess up afterwards. It was the first and last time he was airsick – a baptism by fire that stood him in good stead for the rigours to come. It didn't go so well though, for some of the young WOPs. A few of them suffered so badly from airsickness that they were sent to the Medical Officer and then on to the Medical Board before being classified as unfit for air crew duties. What a mortifying blow – to be re-mustered as ground based wireless operators instead of soaring above the clouds simply because of airsickness. It seemed so unfair to those brave young men, but a sick crew member was a liability and could be a threat to the safety of the aircraft on bombing missions. It seemed an ignominious end to their career, but it had to be done.

CHAPTER ELEVEN

"Bomber country" alias Lincolnshire was the home to many RAF bases – its flat terrain and predominantly rural character being two of its natural advantages. More important, however, was the fact that its strategic location along the eastern seaboard of central England meant that Germany and occupied Europe were within the flying limits of the bombers based there. Conversely, of course, the German *Luftwaffe* could also reach Lincolnshire, and so fighter squadrons were also stationed in the county to provide defensive cover. In March 1943, just before Duncan arrived at RAF Manby on the Lincolnshire coast, there were eleven RAF bomber stations in the county. Four more had opened by the time he dropped his kitbag on the floor in his billet in July. Six months later there were three more. By the end of the war there were over forty,

RAF Manby lay four miles east of the picturesque little market town of Louth. It had opened in 1938 as Number 1 Air Armament School – its purpose being the training of armament officers, bomb aimers, air-gunners and armourers. Duncan's stay there was to be short, just two weeks of ground based training on an Emergency Air Gunnery course. It was intensive work – physically hard, but essential. Originally the wireless operators had performed the dual rôle of gunner and WOP, but as not only the aircraft, but also the operations and the technology had grown ever more complex, the dual rôle had necessarily been split. However, it was still felt wise to give the WOPs an overview of the "nuts and bolts" of air gunnery, so that they could help out should the need arise.

The course was partly theoretical ("air to air" gunnery) but was also heavy on the practical side of things. The novice WOPs had to learn how to operate a Browning machine gun, strip it, clear any stoppages and re-assemble it blind-folded – all in just twelve days. It was hard and challenging work, very different from the more cerebral skills needed by the wireless operator, but the trainees relished it and were duly presented with their air gunner's brevet and sergeant's stripes at the end of the course. It was a proud and fulfilling moment that, for Duncan and his friends, lasted for a mere few hours.

The needle and cotton had been passed from hand to clumsy hand, all of them unused to its subtle fineness – their sergeant's stripes had been sewn with pride on to the coarse fabric of their RAF blue uniforms. Together, the recently "passed out" trainees walked somewhat gingerly toward the unfamiliar territory of the Sergeants' Mess. Their sense of achievement and faint hubris deserted them, however, within moments of entering the building.

"I see you lot have sewed your protection stripes on quickly then" a voice from the back of the room gently mocked Duncan and his pals. The other sergeants who were seated in a group around the man who had called out, all laughed and joined in the friendly mockery. "You sprogs all get your protection stripes up as soon as you can" added a grinning chap with a bushy moustache.

"What do you mean – *protection stripes*?" demanded one of the more confident WOPs.

"Now then, don't get all hot under the collar and airy fairy" replied the man with the moustache. "We're only teasing you young lads. You've got to understand that most of us here have been in the RAF for years. That's how we earned our stripes. You lot have only been on the job for two minutes and you're all decked out. They only give you the stripes so, if you get shot down by Jerry and he picks you up, then you get better treatment because you're an officer."

"They just lock you up and throw away the key instead of shooting you on the spot" added his friend wryly, over a background of friendly cat calls.

Protection stripes. It made sense. Here they all were congratulating themselves on their achievements when in fact the stripes had a far greater significance. It was sobering. The reality of what they were soon about to embark upon was made clearer. And then clearer still, not forty eight hours later, as the strains of the Funeral March echoed forlornly across the runway at Manby. A funeral cortege, each of its coffins draped with a Union Jack, slowly processed toward the main buildings. A plane carrying trainee air gunners had crashed during take-off. All on board were killed before they could even go to war.

There was never any time to stop and think – let alone time to mourn. From Manby, Duncan was posted to RAF Bobbington near Wolverhampton, for Advanced Flying Training working in tandem with trainee navigators. The short training course included arduous, though essential, night flying out over the Irish Sea in Avro Anson aircraft during which the WOPs had to give locational fixes to the navigators that would enable them to plot the course to the target and then return to base. There was much camaraderie in the NAAFI canteen after the training sessions, and it often involved card games. Duncan preferred to watch rather than play, as he didn't like risking his money on cards. However, his passive involvement turned to a rather more active role when a friend asked to borrow a pound note. It was such a lot of money, Duncan would never have gambled with it, but when a friend asks for help, it's a different matter. A pound though. Just a shilling bought an entire week's meat ration. At twenty times that, a whole pound was a great deal of money to lend.

"I'll pay it back the day after tomorrow when we get paid, Dunc. Don't worry. Just let me have it now and you'll get it back, I promise" pleaded his friend.

When payday came, Duncan's friend (and the pound) had gone: posted to another training camp. Duncan was angry with his so-called friend, but even more furious with himself for being such a fool to have lent so much money. Hard earned money. Money that he and Pauline needed desperately. He could never tell her what an idiot he'd been – an absolute halfwit – to have let himself be so easily duped. He'd learned a lesson the hard way. Duncan's spirits hit rock bottom, and of course, his thoughts turned to Pauline for sweet memories to cheer him up. He wanted to see her so much – it was almost a year since they had got married and they'd spent so little time together. He mentioned it to the officer in charge of staff welfare and was overwhelmed when the man replied:

"I can help you sort that out, Sergeant. The housekeeper at the old vicarage takes in servicemen's wives for short stays. I can get it all sorted for you."

Duncan didn't waste a moment. At the first opportunity he wrote to Pauline and told her the good news, begging her to make travel arrangements as soon as possible. It seemed like an eternity before she arrived, though in reality it was only a few days. She was to have a week staying at the vicarage while Duncan continued to undergo training. They were lucky that most of the time while she was there he was on the day time sessions, and he only had one night flying out over the Irish Sea.

The vicarage was a gloomy Victorian building, set back from the road on the edge of Bobbington village. Alongside it was the pretty Holy Cross Church that had its origins in the twelfth century, being much restored in the late 1800s. It was just within walking distance of the RAF base, though despite its proximity the villagers seldom complained of aircraft noise. The sombre appearance of the vicarage was relieved just a fraction by its arched porch and the Arts and Crafts style, stained glass in the front door. Pauline disliked the bleak building intensely. It was cold and dark, with depressing oak furniture, and it was not softened by even a hint of carpeting. She was intimidated by its foreboding melancholy that was matched by the mood of the housekeeper, Grace. On meeting the steely haired matron, Pauline had been severely instructed that she had to keep herself scarce at all times and must absent herself from view if the vicar, the Reverend Griffiths, should appear. Grace had seemed in total awe of the vicar and she imbued Pauline with the same sense of fear (which oddly did not befit a man of the cloth). She was also in awe of her husband, a solemn individual whose only appearance in Pauline's company saw him berating her soundly for putting the knives in the water (as she helpfully washed up after supper) lest their handles should be damaged.

Although Pauline stayed for a week, Duncan was only allowed to leave the base and visit her on three of the nights. Better than nothing, but it made them both ache for more time together. Happy yet sad; bitter yet sweet. Pauline tried to fill her days to keep her mind from straying back to the dwindling time that remained for her in the little village. She trudged down the country lanes, burdened with heavy shopping bags, as she helped the housekeeper to do the weekly shop. They'd had to queue for an hour to get some fish and Pauline was worn out. She tried to think of happier moments to keep her mind off the ache in her shoulders from the weight of the heavy bags and her thoughts turned inevitably to Duncan. She'd confided in him her fears whenever he flew.

"Don't worry, darling," he'd whispered to her last night. "I'll be alright, I promise".

She had to believe him. She had to.

The remainder of Pauline's days were mainly spent playing with the housekeeper's young son, Jackie, a happy-go-lucky young lad of twelve who reminded her of her own brother at that age. She would walk along the surrounding country lanes with him, and run errands, sometimes fetching lettuce and tomatoes from an old chap who sold them from his greenhouse. One afternoon, when the sky had the deep golden tint that reflects the mellowness of late September, the pair went into the orchard behind the vicarage. The plum trees were laden with luscious, deep purple fruits and Jackie stretched up on his tiptoes to pluck one off the pendulous branch. He handed it to Pauline with a shy smile. She was so pretty, yet her eyes looked so sad. The young lad wanted to help her, make her happy, in his own naïve way. The ingenuous gift earned him a sound rebuke from his mother when she discovered what he'd done. Pauline couldn't understand it. The crumpled face of the young lad tugged at her heartstrings and brought tears to her eyes. She tried to defend him, but his mother's anger seemed to be wrapped up with fear. Perhaps the housekeeper was afraid of her master? Whatever the cause, the effect was to sully a gentle and innocent gesture. The taste of the sweet fruit turned sour.

Soon the time came for Pauline to return to Manchester. Just a few days later Duncan, too, left Bobbington, destined for the final stages of his air crew training. It had been a precious time, a jewel of happiness set in a band of pain.

CHAPTER TWELVE

Few who have attended the internationally renowned Grand Prix racing events at the Silverstone race track, would have any inkling of its place in RAF history. Set deep in the idyllic Northamptonshire countryside, Silverstone lies just a short distance away from the glorious National Trust house and gardens of Stowe (also a famous independent school). A few miles to the north of Silverstone is the town of Towcester, while just a few miles to the south in Buckinghamshire, lies Turweston, another location with a place in RAF history. Back in April 1943, RAF Silverstone had opened as Number 17 Operational Training Unit. Before World War Two, air crews had previously completed their operational training on their squadrons. Once war had broken out and operations begun, it was apparent that this could no longer be carried out by units that had become fully active. The answer was to remove some squadrons from active duty and task them with preparing the new crews for operations. They became known as OTUs – Operational Training Units. Silverstone was one such OTU, and it was where Duncan was posted directly after RAF Bobbington.

The first important task at the OTU was to form all the different air crew categories (such as engineers, gunners, wireless operators and so on) into formal flying crews. This was done entirely on a "pick your own" basis, which, somewhat surprisingly, worked extremely well. On paper, this self-selection process (known as crewing up) might seem like an unscientific blend of anarchy and instant compatibility. In practice, however, it worked like a dream. Though entirely undirected, it almost always achieved the desired result of matching up crews based on good vibes – instant empathy and simpatico. All the airmen would assemble in a large hall: the crew leaders (usually the pilots) would start the selection process by walking around the hall and simply asking crew men to join their team. It was really a case of "if your face fits". And it worked incredibly well, as crews chosen in this manner seemed to form strong bonds. National and social barriers were ignored, what mattered was that you'd been picked and now you were part of a team. Your team. Each man would be responsible for the lives of the rest of his crew. They'd train together, fly together, and soon they would face danger and maybe even death together.

The accommodation provided at Silverstone for these new crews was the ubiquitous wooden Nissen huts that were found on many of the newly set up bases; they were comfortable if not luxurious. The airfield itself had three concrete and wood chip runways and there were three massive hangars for the aircraft. The headquarters of the Silverstone RAF base was a large prefabricated structure, and it was here, in October, 1943, where Duncan first met the men who were soon to fly with him and share their best of times and their very worst of times.

First there was Chas.

George Charles Startin looked at the crowd of eager young men milling around the room, and wondered where to begin. The large room inside the squadron headquarters at RAF Silverstone, was only just big enough to hold them all, but at a shade over six foot in height, Chas was able to get a reasonably good view of most of the lads. He shook his head a little, smiling to himself. "If my mum could see me now" he chuckled quietly, making the man standing next to him turn and shoot a quizzical look in his direction. Chas just smiled back – a gentle half smile that lifted the corner of his mouth up just a little on one side. He knew what his mum would say if she really could see him now. She would say how proud she was of him. But she was thousands of miles away, over in Queensland, Australia. As autumn was just beginning here in England, spring was in full bloom for the rest of his family who were half a world away.

Chas was one of many thousands of brave Australians who had left their home country to fly with the British Royal Air Force. He lived to fly. If a person can be born a natural flyer, it was Chas. Since he was a child he had always wanted to be a pilot – to feel the power of the engines at his command, lifting the aircraft, soaring high into the clouds. Now, at twenty four, he had achieved his goal. His training, first with the Royal Australian Air Force and then with the RAF, had been arduous but he had done well, and now he was in the final stage. He had to select his crew carefully so they would work together as a team. "Sort yourselves out, chaps" they'd been told – meaning that they had to group themselves into crews of five. They would be on operations within months now and it was up to the men to form themselves into solid crews who could rely on each other under adverse conditions. The pilots would walk among all the different servicemen in the room, asking first one and then another to join them. As one new crew member and then another was added, the team would build, strengthen and bond until the new unit was formed.

Then there was Ben.

The random mix of men in the room slowly began to show some sort of organization. There were plenty of warm handshakes and genial pats on many broad backs. Chas still didn't know where to start; he cast his eyes around the room again. There were gunners, navigators, bomb aimers, wireless operators. Where to begin? It was very important to him to pick the right team. He needed men who could work together, men who could depend on each other in a crisis. Then he spotted a likely lad – a "Trenchard's brat" – an experienced RAF man who looked like he knew what day it was. His uniform was a little worn, a touch shabby. It didn't have the pristine and proud smartness of the uniform that you mostly saw on the new recruits. Most of them must have been up since 4 a.m. polishing their boots and breathing on their brevets to shine them so they'd look presentable and gain the kudos of being selected right away. But this chap didn't look as if he cared. His hat was a little rakish and showed off his dark, Brylcreemed hair. He looked like he didn't give a damn. He also looked as if he actually knew one end of an aircraft from the other.

"You'll do for me," thought Chas, holding out his hand, palm upward. "I'm Flight Lieutenant Chas Startin. I'm looking for a bomb aimer for my crew, will you join me?"

"Flight Sergeant Keith Lawrence, skipper. Known as Ben to my friends. Happy to join you, skipper, if you'll have me". The young twenty-two year old flashed a grin that showed strong white teeth, a little yellowed by too many recent cigarettes, as he grasped hands firmly with the pilot.

"Ben it is" smiled Chas. "Good to meet you, so that's two of us. We need to find the rest now."

"Right skipper, let's get cracking," laughed Ben, as the two men shook hands once more, cementing a friendship that would last to the very end.

Next came Duncan.

He was standing with a small group of WOp/AGs who had trained together at Bobbington. Chas spotted him first and was drawn by his easy smile and friendly expression – he turned to Ben Lawrence and, nodding toward the small gathering, asked,

"Can you see that group of wireless operators? The fellow with the dark brown hair on the left – he looks as if he'll do. What do you think? "

When Ben had nodded his affirmation, Chas strode up to Duncan and quietly asked,

"Would you like to join us, Sergeant?"

Duncan turned to look at the tall and imposing, dark haired figure. He was struck by the unfamiliar Australian accent that was accompanied by a broad – if somewhat crooked – smile.

"Yes, sir," answered Duncan, without even a second's hesitation. The two men shook hands and moved away from the group of wireless operators. Chas put his hand on Ben Lawrence's shoulder and introduced him to Duncan.

"This is Flight Sergeant Keith Lawrence – but he likes to be called Ben. He's my bomb aimer. I'm Flight Lieutenant Chas Startin, with the Royal Australian Air Force – though I expect you already guessed that from my accent" Chas laughed, a deep rich chuckle. "What's your name, Sergeant?"

"Duncan Freeman, sir. Wireless Operator and Air Gunner. I'm really pleased to join you" Duncan smiled at Chas and then turned to Ben, who gave him a friendly punch on the arm in return.

"Pleased to meet you, Dunc" smiled Ben, a little gruffly.

Duncan looked at the two men; they were like chalk and cheese. The pilot, Chas, was in his mid twenties and was very tall and strongly built, with the quiet, well mannered charm and warmth of a true gentleman. He was neatly groomed and smart, with tanned skin and a very prominent Adam's apple. His Royal Australian Air Force uniform was different to the others, being a deeper, darker blue, and on his shoulders was the proud R.A.A.F. insignia. Ben, on the other hand, was short and well set, with thick, sensual features and dark hair. He had a blasé air and a somewhat rough, self-confident manner that was oddly likeable. He'd joined the RAF some eight years earlier as a trainee, a "Trenchard nipper," and had plenty of experience under his belt.

He'd trained as a pilot in the USA, but with three "pranged" aircraft to his name, it was felt he would be better (and safer) serving as a bomb aimer. A commission had been offered him, but he preferred to stay with the NCOs as one of the lads – it suited his casual, easy-going temperament.

Then they added Ginger.

Chas looked around the room again and said to his two new crew members,

"We'd better get cracking and find our rear gunner and navigator".

"Right skipper" answered Duncan.

"Lead on skip" chimed in Ben, as the trio began to move through the crowd of men. They spotted a group of gunners at the edge of the large room, chatting together and looking around expectantly. Chas turned to Ben and Duncan and asked them if they had any ideas as to which chap to pick. Ben nudged Chas, and said,

"What about that young lad with the ginger hair?"

Chas nodded in agreement and strode forward into the little group.

"Would you like to join us, Sergeant?" he asked the young lad with a warm smile.

The lad turned and smiled gratefully back at Chas. He'd been wondering how long it would be before he was picked, and what the rest of his future crew would be like. He smiled again with relief as he looked at the tall, friendly Australian and the two grinning Sergeants with him.

"Yes please, sir, er… I mean skipper, sir," stammered the young lad, his youthful features crinkling into a grateful grin. The three young men smiled back at him. He was part of their team.

At just eighteen, Eric Hopkinson was one of the youngest airmen in the room, and his fresh-cheeked face shone with his youth and eagerness. His thatch of wavy, strawberry blond hair had been earning him the nickname "Ginger" ever since he was a schoolboy and of course, his RAF colleagues cottoned on to it right away. Eric was an only child who lived with his widowed mother up in Yorkshire, and naturally, she was often on his mind. He knew how proud she was of him and he was looking forward to writing to her to let her know all about how he'd been picked for Chas Startin's crew. Though he was young, barely past boyhood, he knew his job. He'd worked hard during his air gunner's training and he had the rapid physical alertness of youth and a quick reaction response. He was just what Chas needed for their team. One more to go.

And finally Ted.

The last to be picked for Chas's crew and one of the few remaining navigators left unspoken for in the room, Ted Evans hadn't been amongst the highest scorers during his training. He'd worked hard, but it hadn't been easy, and he sometimes wondered if navigation was really the best skill for him to have specialised in. Still, there was no going back now. He was a patriot and he wanted to fight for his country. An affable chap, always friendly and warm, he was pleased when the dark haired Australian pilot had asked him to join his crew. He'd do his best.

And so the five were chosen. The crew had been created and had already bonded through the technique of self-selection. They would stay together and work together, through adversity and danger, to the end. "Per Ardua ad Astra". Through adversity to the stars.

CHAPTER THIRTEEN

The streams of heavy traffic that flood out from the Grand Prix at Silverstone toward the M40 pass close by the derelict control tower on the site of what once was RAF Turweston. If the drivers look across the fields, just a few miles or so before they reach the motorway service station at Cherwell Valley, they might just be able to catch a glimpse of what is today a private airfield lying between Oatleys Farm and the oddly named little river, the Great Ouse. As they sip their café lattes and munch on flaky croissants in the coffee bar at Cherwell Services, few of them could ever realise that back in the 1940s, Wellington bombers operated from the RAF satellite base just a few miles from where their Vauxhall Astras and Mitsubishi Shoguns are parked today.

Turweston formed part of the RAF Silverstone complex; its three concrete runways were put to intense use in 1943 as the twin-engined Vickers Wellington aircraft pounded them day after day. The Wellington was a unique aircraft that had been designed by Barnes Wallace (of the Dam Busters "bouncing bomb" fame). Most air crew fondly called it "The Wimpy" – for its association with the Popeye cartoons that were hugely popular at the time. Spinach-chomping Popeye had a burger-munching friend called J. Wellington Wimpy and of course it doesn't take a leap of the imagination to see how the aircraft earned its nickname. Others also referred to the Wellington bomber as the Flying Cigar owing to the characteristic profile of its fuselage. All air crew, however, seemed to agree on one thing though, and that was the oddly distinctive smell which emanated from the nitrocellulose chemical treatment (called "dope") that was used to tighten and harden the linen outer skin of the aircraft.

The Wellington had a unique design that made it very strong yet also somewhat vulnerable. Its fuselage was a geodetic lattice work construction of interlocking triangles, similar to the rigid construction of early airships (which Barnes Wallace had also designed). This type of honeycomb metal construction made the aircraft very tough and durable, lightweight yet strong at the same time, and it often survived the sort of battle damage that would have destroyed other aircraft. Chunks of it could even be shot away and the plane would still remain airworthy. However, the doped surface was also very flammable – a fact that surely was in the minds of many young airmen.

Chas Startin and his crew had been assigned to Turweston for training on the medium sized bombers. Before the full crew could make their first operational flight, however, Chas needed experience on the Wellingtons, as these bigger bombers were new to him. First there were a couple of trial flights (called "dickey flights") with experienced crews before taking his own crew up by himself. Then there were circuits and bumps – a most descriptive way of describing pilot training in which repeated take offs and landings resulted in constant circling above the airfield. Although it was only an exercise, there was always danger, especially when flying at night. A few months earlier, at the RAF airfield of Little Horwood just a few miles away on the other side of the market town of Buckingham, a Wellington on circuits and bumps had hit a water tower while coming in to land. All four crew on board had been killed instantly. Chas had heard about the crash on the Mess grapevine and it helped him to concentrate hard as he brought the aircraft into its final approach at Turweston. The Aldis lamp held by the runway controller was glowing green, indicating that the plane had clearance to land, as Chas safely negotiated the Wellington onto the ground. He exhaled slowly and began to taxi the aircraft toward the waiting ground crew on the aerodrome's perimeter track. Soon he would be taking to the air with his own crew on their first semi-operational flight. Their lives would be in his hands. His hands. Chas looked down at them, encased in dark leather gauntlets over a pair of fine, silk gloves. He rested his hands on the control column and looked up, taking in the velvet darkness of the night. His childhood dream of becoming a pilot had been turned into harsh reality. The months of training, practicing steep turns, spins, forced landings and evasive action were now all behind him. Chas knew that, as a bomber pilot, he didn't need to excel in aerobatics; he needed to always remain calm to the point of being nerveless. Ability, training, teamwork and sheer determination were the qualities that were needed now. The future, though unknown, held some grim certainties that he preferred not to dwell on. His mind leapt months and miles as the bittersweet memory of his mother's tears filled his head. She had clasped him to her tightly as they had bid each other farewell, her eyes brimming over with the tears she had tried so hard to hide. The memory of his father's voice, gruff with emotion, saying "we're proud of you, son". Chas blinked and swallowed hard, trying to nudge the precious memory from his mind. Right now he needed to be strong; he needed to stay calm.

The Wellingtons were operated by a full crew of six, and so an extra man had to be found. Chas's crew was made up of Ben, the bomb aimer; Dunc, the wireless operator; Ted, the navigator and Ginger, the rear gunner. The sixth member of the crew now needed, was a mid-upper gunner and a twenty four year old fellow from Lurgan in Northern Ireland called Ernie McIlwaine, filled the slot. The team strengthened: the five became six. The family grew.

Together they worked through yet more training. Preparation for ditching in the sea took place in the gentle waters of the local swimming baths – a far cry from the cold, grey swell of the North Sea. Duncan had always enjoyed swimming, so it was a piece of cake for him, even weighed down by the sodden trousers and jackets they all had to wear in the water. Not so for poor Ginger who couldn't swim at all. Desperate to hide his fear as well as his inexperience, he dog paddled through the water and hauled himself exhausted into the inflatable life raft. Synchronised boarding of the unstable raft was essential, and Duncan carefully timed his own moves to match Ginger's flailing, so that the full crew all managed to get on board successfully. False confidence in their achievement was perhaps better than the certain knowledge of what ditching in the North Sea would actually present.

Parachute training, too, was carried out in uncharacteristic (and reasonably unchallenging) surroundings, with no time for the niceties of jumping out of an aircraft. Temporary scaffolding around seven or eight foot tall, provided the height necessary for jumping practice. The airmen, fully kitted up so that they could familiarise themselves with the feel of the parachute webbing, took turns at jumping off and landing correctly. The urgencies of war meant that more air crew were needed immediately; losses in the air had been immense. There was simply no time to provide more formal training with on-the-spot experience. Nevertheless, even this cursory training boosted the men's morale. The unknown became less fearful through a semblance of familiarity.

The tension mounted. They were young; they were fit and strong. They'd trained till they were weary with the very training itself. They longed to fight for their King and their country. Patriotism coursed through every vein in every body. They were ready – and yet. There was just a tiny frisson of fear. A butterfly of a thing, that fluttered past and brushed against their young cheeks when they least expected it to. It went unrecognised by many who protested that they were not afraid. But in dreams, the spectre could no longer be controlled. In dreams, fear took form.

Soon, it would not only be in their dreams.

By the end of October, 1943, Duncan and his fellow crew members were ready. Their first call came soon; though they were still strictly in training (for the crew had not yet been "converted" to the heavy bombers) their first semi-operational flight would be no picnic, for it was to be a "nickel" raid over occupied France, to drop propaganda leaflets. Nickelling (leaflet dropping) was a task that was often given to new crews who hadn't been on operations before, as a means of gently introducing them to the theatre of war. Gently? Can such things ever be done gently? Occupied France was dangerous terrain to be flying over and many aircraft had been lost on similar ops. The crew was briefed; this was for real. On November 5th, 1943, Flight Lieutenant Chas Startin and his crew of five boarded their Wellington bomber at RAF Silverstone in Northamptonshire and set course for Orleans, in northern France.

CHAPTER FOURTEEN

The sound of violent retching could be heard over the roar of the Hercules engines. The noise became even louder as Duncan fought his way down the fuselage of the Wellington towards the gun turret. Then the vomiting began. As Duncan looked up into the gun turret he could see the faint light of the crescent moon on Ernie McIlwaine's white face. He looked very sick indeed. Ernie retched again and vomited, as Duncan quickly stepped back and out of the line of fire.

"The Skipper said you'd called him on the intercom, Ernie – he asked me to come and see how you are. Let me help you out" Duncan shouted at the ashen figure above him, raising his voice to be heard above the engines. "Come down, you're no use to us in that condition. Come and lie down, you'll feel better soon".

McIlwaine retched again, his body tensing with the pain. He hunched forward as much as was possible in the confined space of the gun turret to unbuckle himself from the canvas sling on which he was seated.

"I'm coming Dunc," he gasped between retches. Duncan reached out and steadied him, guiding him back into the main body of the Wellington's fuselage.

"I'm so... oh not again..." the gunner bent double and groaned. "So sorry Dunc... I think it's the smell and the turbulence, that's done it".

He retched again, a stomach churning sound that combined with the acid stench of vomit and the nauseating reek of the Wellington bomber's dope to make Duncan feel like throwing up too. He steeled himself and tried to concentrate on helping his friend onto the rest bed. The gunner was kitted out in a flying suit that was electrically heated to keep him warm in his exposed position in the turret. He'd removed his oxygen mask while vomiting, and was now feebly attempting to clasp it back to his face and gulp in its comparative freshness. He lay down on the bed and again felt the desire to apologise for his weakness.

"I'm sorry Dunc".

Ernie felt bad at letting down the rest of the crew – of not pulling his weight. They were his friends, his comrades, they were all in it together, and this was their first real flight over enemy territory, even though it didn't count as an operation in the strict sense of the word – their load was only paper leaflets, not bombs. Camaraderie is an essential quality for any group working together, but never was it more vital or more strong than for the crews on board the aircraft of Bomber Command. Each man had his job, and each man was dependant on the others. They were sharing the same dangers and the same fears. Their morale was that of the group rather than the individual. They were a close-knit unit, a team, in every sense of the word. Duncan could sense McIlwaine's frustration and despair at letting his friends down, but a sick team member was a useless one.

"Ernie, you don't need to say you're sorry. We know you are. There's no point in staying at your post if you're ill and can't do the job. The Skip' wants you out of the turret and resting on the bed. Look, I can't stay any longer here, I've got to get back to the wireless. You'll be alright soon, chum".

Duncan grasped the mask attached to his oxygen cylinder and tried to draw a breath from it. The gauge showed the cylinder was full, but there wasn't as much as a lung-full coming from it. He let the mask drop and breathed in as deeply as he could. It wasn't easy. The Wellington was flying at around ten thousand feet, so there was just enough oxygen in the air around him, but even so his chest felt sore and tight. They were over northern France now and should soon be approaching their target area of

Orleans. It was important that he got back to the wireless set at his work station, there were things he needed to do quickly as his job on this mission also involved releasing the payload of leaflets. Finishing his tasks on the R1154 wireless receiver, Duncan moved down the aircraft to the flare chute and the waiting stack of leaflets that would shortly be dropped. He heard the crackling voice of the bomb aimer, Ben, over the intercom wired into his flying helmet. "Five minutes to target". Five minutes still, so he had a moment or two – he pulled a leaflet out of the string-tied bundle and studied it. The familiar red and blue RAF roundels adorned the banner title: *"Le Courrier de l'Air" apporte par la RAF. Londres, le 28 Octobre 1943.* [The Mail of the Air, brought by the RAF. London, 28th October, 1943.]

The four page flimsy was full of news aimed to cheer the French, telling of battles won and ground gained. The crackling on the intercom stirred Duncan back to action.

"Approaching target…"

Duncan filled the chute with the papers – the bundles rushed down, freefalling their way through the dark night to the Loire Valley and Orleans, thousands of feet below. Now came the moment Duncan was dreading. Count to eight and fire the photo flare into the chute immediately after the leaflets to record their drop. The smell of dope – flammable dope – was everywhere in the Wellington. A flare going off too soon in the chute, perhaps if any of the leaflets hadn't quite cleared it, or worse, maybe got stuck, would surely have meant an instant and catastrophic fire. Duncan held his breath as he fired the flare; seconds passed. It seemed forever. But there was nothing but a whistling silence from the flare chute. They'd done it, now to get back home. Safely.

On their route out to Orleans, the Wellington had experienced a burst of anti aircraft fire (flak) from the German defences positioned on the French coast. It had been brief and hadn't caused too much consternation amongst the "rookie" crew. Ginger Hopkinson, the tail end gunner, had been constantly watching out for enemy aircraft, but they weren't a threat on this op. Now the Wellington had to negotiate the coastal defences again, and this time they could well be alert to the threat of returning aircraft; they could be ready and watching for them. The crew had talked among themselves via the intercom system on the outward leg of the journey to the target; it had helped to alleviate the nervousness they all felt during their first flight over enemy terrain. Now, on the return leg, they were silent; the static crackling on the intercom being punctuated with the sounds of breathing interspersed by an occasional essential message.

As they neared the Channel coast and the flak batteries, the tension inside the aircraft became palpable. Duncan concentrated on his tasks at the radio to keep his mind off the threat. Ginger stayed alert in the rear gun turret while Ben, the bomb aimer, kept his eyes open for any sign of the batteries opening fire. A sudden burst of yellow flashes ahead of them let them know their fears had been correct. A strong smell of cordite permeated the aircraft from the exploding shells in the air around them. Chas gritted his teeth and breathed slowly, as he piloted the aircraft through clouds of black smoke. The real danger was if they were right above or to the side of the explosion: so far so good. Another burst, brighter, stronger. Still they flew. All six men in the Wellington held their breath and prayed. Then Ginger's excited voice over the intercom;

"Flak burst behind us, Skip".

Chas's hands were steady on the throttles, as the two Hercules engines droned on, carrying the Wellington steadily but surely away from the worst of the flak. The night sky was dark, no further fireworks. Relief flooded over Chas and his shoulders relaxed a little as the tension lessened. In the rear turret, Ginger stopped trembling, telling himself that it was just the cold that was giving him the shivers. Ben looked up from his post and gave Chas a "thumbs up" and a wry smile. Ernie still in the grips of nausea simply sighed. All was not quite so well in the navigator's station, however, and Duncan didn't share in the sudden relief that the others were enjoying as he was beginning to realise that a new danger was presenting itself. Ted, the navigator, seemed to be in a panic. His head was bobbing wildly and he was moving sheets of paper from side to side. He looked across at the instruments and then moaned. Duncan got up and tapped him on the shoulder. The navigator jumped, startled, and turned to Duncan, his eyes wild.

"I... I... don't know where we are," he hissed under his breath.

"What!?" replied Duncan, incredulously.

"I don't know. We're somewhere, somewhere, well, here I think..." The navigator waved his hand vaguely over the map.

"Are you serious?" asked Duncan, his face ashen.

The navigator nodded. "I'm sorry, I've lost our bearings. I'm sorry."

Duncan knew he had to act quickly and alert the rest of the crew to the problem, but first he needed to switch on the Identification Friend or Foe (IFF) system, as he realised they would soon be approaching the south coast of England. It certainly would be an irony if they were to be shot down by their own guns after having escaped the recent flak attack. He moved to his workstation as he spoke into the intercom.

"Skipper, we've got a bit of a problem here. The navigator's clueless as to where we actually are right now. Looks like Ben and I will have to box clever and work something out between us. I can keep taking radio bearings – that ought to guide us back to Silverstone. Can Ben watch out below and fix some locations for us?"

There was a momentary silence among the entire crew as the enormity of Duncan's message sank in. They were effectively lost, with just enough fuel to get them back to their base by a direct flight path. Ben's voice broke the silence.

"We can do it, Skipper. There's just enough dawn light now for me to see the channel, we must be approaching Blighty soon".

Chas took control, his tone light and steady.

"Yes. Agreed. That's the way we'll do it, Duncan. Ben, keep me informed as to what you see below. Duncan, keep taking the radio bearings. The weather's clear, we can make it. Press on regardless, chaps".

Ted, the navigator, sat with his head in his hands – sick at his failure. Duncan was too busy to pay attention to him.

"I can see the English coast. It looks like the Isle of Wight" shouted Ben. The island's distinctive shape appeared below him almost as if he had simply turned over the pages of his old school atlas – Mercator projection. "We're right on course".

A tiny shiver of relief ran over the crew. At least they were over familiar territory now. The Wellington droned on: four of its crew intent on their tasks, concentrating hard; the remaining two passive – one still nauseous and now sleeping, the other wretched at his personal failure. The staccato sounds of Morse code punctuated the intermittent silences, and between times, Duncan relayed the information he was getting via the radio bearings to Chas and Ben. Isolated in the tail end of the aircraft, Ginger prayed that his fellow crew members were getting it right. He could see the winter countryside in the pale early morning light, thousands of feet below him. A patchwork of brown and grey fields, here and there dotted with fingers of civilization. Hills and ridges, their steepness standing out in relief, came into view. The Hampshire Downs, the Chilterns. Still the aircraft flew on. The radio bearings had been sound; the aircraft reached the circuit area of RAF Silverstone and came in to land by visual sighting. As the wheels touched the runway, the sheer relief on board the Wellington was palpable.

Their pleasure was short lived.

They had landed at RAF Turweston instead of RAF Silverstone.

CHAPTER FIFTEEN

The entire crew had felt dreadfully embarrassed when they had had to fly from Turweston back to their home base of RAF Silverstone, later that day. But none had felt it more than Chas. His first official flight over enemy territory and he couldn't bring the ruddy kite back to the correct RAF base. He was dismayed with the poor performance of his navigator, but even more annoyed with himself. Typical of Chas, he blamed himself for choosing Ted, feeling that he should have known the man's shortcomings. "How could I have known?" he asked himself, between bouts of self-flagellation over the entire embarrassing affair. Ted had performed so well during exercises, he had seemed so proficient and capable. But under fire, in the air, when the pressure was on, he'd gone to pieces. Simply couldn't cope.

There had been several words said during the debriefing at Silverstone. The navigator had been reprimanded and the other pilots had had a lot of fun ribbing Chas.

"At least you found the right country. Sure you weren't trying to make it back to Oz?"

He could take it, they meant well, but it smarted. On the other hand, as he looked back at the entire incident, Chas realised just how well the core members of his crew had reacted to the emergency. Duncan and Ben had worked with him to overcome the problem and to get them all back home. Ginger had pitched in too, as much as he possibly could. Considering it was their first flight over enemy territory, he realised that he was actually very proud of them. There'd been no panic, never even a hint of fear, just a solid determination to see the job through together as best as possible. He smiled. His crew – they'd helped each other and worked together as one. Yes, they made a good team. It was strange, but they were beginning to feel more like family than crew members.

They'd all been teased too; Chas wasn't the only one that had been subject to it. In the Sergeant's Mess the following day, there'd been a number of references to those "protection stripes" from the more experienced men.

"You'd have needed those stripes if you'd ended up putting your kite down amongst the frogs" said one chap, chuckling to himself. Duncan, Ben and Ginger exchanged glances and grimaced. It wasn't their fault, but they took the comments with reluctant good grace.

"I hear your navigator got torn off a strip" remarked another man. "Aw, don't look so browned off. You lot coped well from what I hear. Your pilot was saying that you did a good job getting your Wimpy back. He was singing your praises."

"Cheer up, lads. Go and get yourself some char and a wad. You'll feel a lot better when your stomach's filled".

It was sound advice. The trio went off to buy a halfpenny cake and a cup of strong tea. The cake (known as a wad) was a rockbun, stodgy and somewhat hard; in fact the name "rockbun" conjured up exactly the right sensation to describe the ensuing encounter between tooth and cake. The Mess was buzzing with activity and Duncan recalled, red-faced, the meal they'd had the previous day, just after they returned back to base. He'd found a large grub inside his potato, and he foolishly drew the attention of the Mess' Orderly Sergeant to it. The man had looked down at Duncan and completely ignored his complaint. Duncan had felt stupid and a little humiliated. He realised how raw and inexperienced he must seem to these older RAF men. Duncan and Ginger were new boys, wearing their stripes with pride, yet they'd only been in the RAF for a short while. Their smart new blue-grey overcoats and fresh faces marked them out as sprogs – newcomers.

Duncan fingered the rockbun and took a bite, washing it down with a gulp of hot, strong tea. The taste of the cake took his mind back to the previous year; to the day he married Pauline. He recalled the ersatz cake she'd made as if it was only yesterday. He missed her so much. The ache inside him, as he recalled their wedding and how beautiful she had looked, was a physical pain. What was she doing now? Was she thinking of him? Was she worrying, listening to the wireless and reading the newspapers? Was she well; was she taking care of herself? He was helpless to do anything beyond write to her whenever he had time.

Communication. We take it for granted today. With our mobile phones and our instant internet access, it's so easy to stay in touch. It's hard to imagine, if your only experience is of today's fast paced world, how difficult it was for families to stay in contact throughout the war years with their loved ones who were in service. And how eagerly greeted was the postman. Unless of course, he was delivering the most feared communication of all, the official telegram, bearing those terrible words – "killed in action".

CHAPTER SIXTEEN

Christmas 1943: meat, cheese, sugar, tea, margarine, butter and plenty more daily foodstuffs were rationed. Many other previously staple foods were in short supply. Crazy things happened. A single banana was offered as a prize in an office raffle while queues over a mile long formed outside one shop when word got out that cooking apples were available there. Shortages were at their height; there was little chance of turkey, chicken or goose for the Christmas table. A family would count itself lucky if it had a bit of mutton as festive fare. Scraps of greenery collected from the hedgerows (if you were lucky enough to have any nearby) sufficed for decoration, while a candle in a plant pot served as a Christmas tree for many.

Christmas presents were hard to come by – even paper to wrap them in was impossible to get. The perennial favourites – sweets and toilet soap – had been added to the lengthening list of rationed goods, so home-made "this and that" – gloves, scarves, slippers – appeared in many Christmas stockings instead.

But for most people, the real gift, the only gift they wanted and desired, was to have their loved ones with them. For Pauline and Duncan, Christmas 1943 brought them that joy, for Duncan was granted a short leave. Precious time was spent travelling, kit bag slung over his shoulder; but that time passed quickly with growing anticipation, as Duncan's train drew ever nearer to Manchester.

Pauline had been living in a dilapidated one room flat, but had moved back to her parents' home on doctor's orders after she'd lost weight through a combination of too little food and too much worry. Her appearance startled and troubled Duncan when he saw her as she waited for him at the station. He was somewhat re-assured by the fact that at least she wasn't living by herself now, but that brought with it the less pleasant knowledge that they would be staying together in the attic of Pauline's parents' house while he was on leave.

Stiflingly hot in the summer, the attic was the complete opposite in mid winter. While Duncan was away, Pauline had been sharing her sister's room, but now that her husband was home on leave, the attic had been partially cleared to make way for a bed and a small chest of drawers. It was bitterly cold and smelled strongly of the pigeons that also "called" it home. But it was theirs, for just a few short, precious days. They sat together, hands clasped tightly, trying to hold the moment forever, as the wireless quietly serenaded them with the familiar words "I'm dreaming of a white Christmas". As the song ended, the strains of Adamson and McHugh's recent song "Comin' in on a Wing and a Prayer" drifted across the chilly room. Duncan stole a glance at Pauline, she smiled. Together they joined in the chorus:

"With our full crew aboard
And our trust in the Lord
We're comin' in on a wing and a prayer".

They laughed at their amateurish efforts at harmony, only to fall silent moments later at the implications of the song.

"I'll be alright" whispered Duncan, in reply to Pauline's unspoken question. She lowered her head. How else could you hide tears?

On the day after Boxing Day, Duncan shouldered his kit bag again and gritted his teeth. They say "parting is such sweet sorrow" but to him it was all sorrow with none of the sweetness. In fact it was agony to leave his young wife, but duty called. King and Country called. And in many thousands upon thousands of homes, in countries on both sides of the war, young men and women were bidding farewell to those they loved. Mothers hid their weeping, fathers stood tall, as those who must take their leave gave one final glance and prayed that it would not be their last.

As he sat in the cold carriage of the train bound for Lincolnshire, Duncan's thoughts turned to his friends, the other members of his crew. He knew Ginger had gone home for Christmas, back to see his Mum in Yorkshire, Ben was with his own young wife and Ernie had gone home too. But Chas couldn't get back home to Australia on such a short leave, so he had gone to visit some family friends in northern England.

Duncan wondered if Ginger would still be pining for the scruffy dog that he'd found while they were stationed at Silverstone. It was a black Labrador and had appeared to be homeless, whining whenever it came near Ginger and staring up at him with doleful eyes. Ginger had become devoted to it within days, and he had sneaked it into their Nissen hut billet where its whining had given everyone disturbed nights. He'd called the Labrador Nipper and fed it on scraps from the NAAFI canteen, spending every moment of his spare time playing with it. The rest of the lads had teased him, but he hadn't cared. The dog had given him more than just a bit of fun, it had also provided a touch of comfort, a reminder of the softer, gentler side of life. Of days when he was a lad in Wakefield, playing with his friends in the park (they called it "laking about"). There'd been an old grey mongrel that used to appear whenever Ginger and his young friends started kicking a football around. The dog would run around crazily after the ball, barking and then chasing its tail when it became frustrated with the lads' antics. Nipper reminded him of his childhood, it seemed so long ago yet it was only a few short years.

The train rumbled along with a familiar clickety-clack rhythm. It was almost soporific, but the intense chill inside the unheated carriage put a stop to any thoughts of sleep. The train was packed with people, many of them service men and women returning back to their bases after Christmas. Duncan looked outside at the cold, barren landscape of Saddleworth Moor, as the train rattled along, climbing slowly toward the Woodhead tunnel. He smiled wryly to himself, causing the old fellow on the opposite seat to wonder what on earth the airman sitting across from him could possibly have to smile at. In fact, Duncan's thoughts were still with Ginger, and the smile was one of pity and sadness, as he recalled his friend's intense sorrow when the Labrador had been killed. It had been a shock to them all – though Duncan had felt silly to be upset at the loss of a dog when men and women, children and babies, were being blown to pieces every day. Nevertheless it had been a disturbing incident. The poor dog had scampered off toward the perimeter track at Silverstone and got itself flattened by one of the trucks. Ginger had been inconsolable at first. His babyish features had crumpled, and he had looked even younger than his eighteen years as he had fought back the tears. Chas had gone out of his way to try and help, and the rest of them had done their best to take Ginger's mind off the poor old dog. But it hadn't been easy, he had felt its loss keenly, and Duncan hoped that a few days at home with his Mum and his old friends might have helped Ginger to get his mind round things.

Blackness descended on the carriage as the train entered the three-mile long tunnel on its way from Manchester to Sheffield. No one seemed startled, they were all used to blackouts in this fourth year of hostilities, but the acrid smell of smoke and other fumes that permeated the carriage wasn't so welcome. A glimmer of yellow light came from the weak lamps over the doors;

Duncan leaned back as much as was possible on the uncomfortable seats, and sighed. They would all be back together again soon, at Scampton, where they were to wait until they were posted on to the Heavy Conversion Unit at RAF Wigsley. Already, the days at Christmas spent with Pauline were a memory. How fast time flies when you are happy. It was a cliché, but painfully true. Duncan screwed up his eyes as the train emerged from the Pennine tunnel and the harsh light of the bleak winter's day took the passengers by surprise. He blinked as his eyes adjusted to the brightness. Reality beckoned.

CHAPTER SEVENTEEN

The first heavy snows of 1944 fell on Sunday January 16th. It was a major problem for the RAF as runways had to be cleared and aircraft made ready for operations. All ranks, from the very highest to the very lowest, were given the task of shovelling the thick blanket of snow off the runways. It was heavy work and bitterly cold, but absolutely essential to keep operations running. Many of the Australians in the crews had never seen snow before, and so at first it was something of a novelty to them. They'd grasped the shovels and brooms with gusto, and there had been a number of snowball fights when the officers weren't looking. But the bitter cold eventually got through to everyone and, still shivering from the biting wind, the men would crowd into the canteen when their shift was over and clasp their raw, red fingers round hot cups of steaming tea.

Bliss.

Now in their final stages of training, Chas's crew had several postings during those first, bitterly cold, ten weeks of the year. All were in Lincolnshire – Bomber Country. There'd been the Heavy Conversion Unit at RAF Wigsley, where they "converted" to (became familiarised with) the heavy four engined bombers, instead of the smaller two engines that they had trained on so far. Chas was soon flying Stirling bombers and a new member of the team – the flight engineer – was added to his crew. The four engined heavy bombers were more complex, and it was impossible for the pilot alone to control all four engines as well as fly the plane. The engineer's prime rôle was to monitor the engines and fuel consumption, as well as act as an assistant on many other tasks such as take-off and landing. A twenty year old Irish lad from County Cork, called "Paddy" Duggan, joined

Chas's crew as flight engineer, and a new navigator, Pilot Officer Francis Linton from the Royal Canadian Air Force, came on board to replace the disgraced Ted Evans. At thirty two, Linton was a decade older than the rest of the crew and he'd left a wife back home on the other side of the "pond". He was an amiable guy, and everyone straight away called him "Nav".

Early in March, the snow storms returned to Lincolnshire, enveloping everything in a dense blanket of white. At the RAF aerodromes, all the personnel were pressed into action again, with every implement and tool that could be used to shift the snow off the runways and perimeter roads. Chas and his crew had also spent some time training at windswept RAF Swinderby, just outside Newark in Lincolnshire. The landscape was very flat and the aerodrome was exposed to the biting easterly winds that had brought yet more heavy snow to the county. The airmen had broken off from their training to help with the intensive snow clearing operations, but not for long. From Swinderby they were moved on to RAF Syerston, Number 5 Group Lancaster Finishing School, where air crews received the final specific training needed to fly the massive Lancaster bombers.

Duncan had been especially intrigued and deeply focused on the training he'd received at Swinderby for the new "Monica" tail warning radar system. The idea was that it alerted the wireless operator to enemy aircraft approaching from behind or below and was effective over an area of about four miles. Later critics would point to the fact that enemy aircraft soon became fitted with a method of homing in on the "Monica" pulses. It was a double-edged sword. However, it seemed a damned fine invention to the air crew, as it was the only means of spotting attacking enemy aircraft coming at them from those directions that were otherwise impossible to detect. Duncan become proficient at reading and operating the "Monica" system, hoping that he would never need it, yet knowing that he undoubtedly would.

Necessity is so often "the mother of invention" and it was undoubtedly necessity that brought about the advancement of radar and navigational systems during the late 1930s and early 1940s. One such radio navigation system that was developed (based on the familiar principle of triangulation) was known as "Gee". Three transmitters (the "trinity") sent out a synchronised radio pulse at precise intervals – and by comparing the time at which each pulse arrived on his receiver, the navigator could then check a chart and calculate the position of his aircraft very accurately. It thus enabled the navigator to follow a set course and know the aircraft's position on track to its target.

The "Gee" system got its name from the electronic grid (G for grid) of latitude and longitude that was effectively generated by the combination of the three signals received by the aircraft. Bad weather couldn't interfere with the signals, and the use of "Gee" proved an enormous benefit to Bomber Command. It did have a couple of problems though: it was fairly short range and so could not extend over the radio horizon, though it was very effective over mainland Britain, and the North Sea. Its other main problem was that it could be jammed by enemy aircraft, but that was a price that had to be paid. Today's familiar Global Positioning System (GPS) that many people use for in-car navigation, evolved out of the "Gee" technology.

The aircraft that Chas and his crew had so far flown were equipped with the "Gee" system; soon they were to fly on Lancasters that would similarly be equipped with "Gee". The effective range on the Lancaster was greater than other bombers such as the Halifax, because they were able to fly at a higher altitude and thus stay in range for longer. But once out of range of the transmitters, the navigator needed to be able to calculate and measure to such a degree that he could pinpoint the position of the aircraft while in flight without any external aid. This was known as Dead Reckoning – the process of estimating where the aircraft will be at a certain time if you hold the speed, time and course you plan to travel.

In 1942, a special target finding force had been set up. Called the Pathfinders, they were a group of elite crews who flew ahead of the main bombing forces, and marked the targets with coloured flares or other indicators. Their aircraft (often, but not always, lighter and faster) were equipped with the very latest navigational aids – and the one that really made a difference was the oddly named H2S. This was the main search radar equipment that provided the navigator with a form of pictorial representation of the ground beneath the aircraft. Features such as water, buildings and roads showed up clearly. Like both "Gee" and "Monica", H2S was a double-edged sword. It had the advantage that it could not be jammed, but it had the disadvantage that specially-equipped *Luftwaffe* night-fighters could home in on the aircraft that used it. A trade-off. You couldn't have one without the other. Crossed fingers and lucky talismans were also part of the necessary equipment for RAF air crew.

Several explanations can be found for the intriguing name H2S. Maybe someone, somewhere, knows which is the correct version. One story tells of an officer who was visiting the factory where the navigational units were being built. When he was told about the device's expected performance, he was critical and reputedly said:

"It stinks, so call it H_2S ".

The chemical symbol for hydrogen sulphide is H_2S, its smell is better known as that of rotten eggs!

Another story tells that the initial acronym for the radar system was TF, standing for Town Finder. Legend has it that an officer was livid that such an easy to guess acronym was being used, and he said, angrily, that it stank. H2S again, those rotten eggs!

A more pleasant and fragrant explanation is that H2S stands for "Home Sweet Home" Two Hs and one S. The link being that the radar system was a device that would enable the crew to complete their mission and find their way back to home, sweet home. Yet another rational explanation for the acronym is that it stood for Height to Slope (a layman's version of its *modus operandi*).

There's no speculation however, regarding what H2S was, and how it originated. The noted scientist, Sir Bernard Lovell of Jodrell Bank fame, had been tasked with developing an airborne, targeting radar system. His team included an especially brilliant man, Alan Blumlein, who was responsible for developing the electronic circuitry involved. There are always setbacks involved in any development programme, but an especially savage one blighted this team. On the afternoon of June 7th, 1942, a Halifax bomber took off from RAF Defford in Worcestershire to perform a series of airborne tests on the prototype H2S system. During airborne trials, at just after four in the afternoon, one of the engines of the Halifax caught fire. The aircraft crashed onto a field near the village of Welsh Bicknor in Herefordshire, damaging the prototype H2S and the highly secret Magnatron device that was at its heart. All on board perished including three of the leading scientists. One of the dead was Alan Blumlein.

His body, along with those of the other ten men, lay on the hillside over night, for the recovery of the top secret equipment had to take precedence. Back in London, Blumlein's wife, Doreen, and his two young sons, Charles and David, wept with grief. Alan Blumlein was a genius, and arguably the greatest British electronics engineer of the 20th century, credited with the invention of stereo sound systems, as well as other major contributions to the development of recording and television and of course, the electronic wizardry behind the H2S radar system. To quote Robert Alexander, Blumlein's biographer, "if you have lived in the 20th century and listened to and enjoyed music reproduced from record or CD, if you watched television or travelled safely in an aeroplane from one country to another, then the life and work of Alan Blumlein has touched you; for it was he who made these things – and more – possible."

One can only wonder what else Blumlein might have offered the world had his brief sweet life not been brought to such an untimely end on that warm June afternoon. And one can only wonder how many lives his genius in the sphere of radar, must have saved.

CHAPTER EIGHTEEN

The leaves were just beginning to show on the ash trees in the Old Wood when the heavy lorries turned off the B 1190 and rumbled along the aerodrome's perimeter road, finally coming to a halt outside the main admin block at RAF Skellingthorpe. Chas and his crew, along with several other groups of airmen, had arrived at their new base – the home of 50 Squadron, part of the illustrious No. 5 Group. Spring had begun to touch the trees in the woods that ringed the airfield, despite the recent heavy snows and the late March air felt cool and fresh.

The landscape was flat and interrupted only by the gentle profile of the trees in the scattered woodlands. On their way to the airfield, most of the airmen had noticed the golden towers of Lincoln Cathedral, magnificent against the pale blue sky. The Cathedral, situated on the top of Lindum Hill, could be seen for twenty miles over the flat Lincolnshire fenland. A cathedral had been on the site since William the Conqueror had ordered construction to begin in 1072. Savage fires and then, astonishingly, an earthquake had brought about the destruction of subsequent edifices over the ensuing two centuries. In the 1200s, the current structure was completed, though there have been many alterations and much re-modelling since then.

RAF Skellingthorpe was situated near the village of the same name, and just a few miles from the city of Lincoln. There were a number of bomber airfields in the area, but Skellingthorpe (known as Skelly to the RAF men and women) was the closest to the city. All RAF airfields were given a two letter reference, known as a pundit code. Skellingthorpe's was FG. The purpose was to help air crews navigate back to their base, and the code was sent to incoming aircraft, in Morse, from a beacon situated around five miles away from each airfield. It was a new airbase, built (just a few years before Chas and his crew arrived) on open pasture known locally as Black Moor, to relieve the pressure on nearby RAF Waddington.

Three hard concrete and tarmac runways were laid down at Skelly, strong enough to withstand the incessant pounding they would receive from the heavy bombers. To allow for greater flexibility, the three runways were arranged in a triangle shape, thus allowing take off and landing from six different directions according to operational needs, weather conditions and so on. Around the perimeter of the airfield were the 'frying pan' shaped aircraft dispersals that allowed for the planes to be effectively parked, and made sure, as far as possible, that no aircraft would be an immediate danger to another. By not grouping the waiting aircraft together, this further ensured that any air attack would be less likely to find easy targets of clustered aircraft. Accommodation and communal facilities for over two thousand service men and women was also constructed on the site.

And what aircraft awaited Chas and his six fellow crew members at RAF Skellingthorpe, when they joined the ranks of 50 Squadron, that gentle March day in 1944? The mighty Avro Lancaster.

Many aircraft have been immortalised by history. Their legacy being that they have, on many levels, touched people's lives. The elegant Concorde, the dashing Spitfire, the majestic Hercules and so many more. But possibly no single aircraft has gained a greater fame than the mighty Lancaster. Crewed by thousands upon thousands of volunteers; brave young men, from every walk of life. Shop keepers, miners, managers, milkmen, carpenters, mechanics, teachers, postmen, students, clerks and more. They were taken from their everyday lives and trained to become pilots, engineers, wireless operators, navigators, bomb aimers and gunners. Their average age was just twenty two. They were spurred on by either bravery or bravado (and only some of them had the wisdom, or experience, to know the difference). Thousands upon thousands of brave young men met their end on board that mighty aircraft. Thousands more still lived on to tell their tale.

This is their legacy. This is their story.

Cramped and awkward working conditions, precious little defensive armour, an all pervasive smell of metal, oil and aviation fuel, throbbing vibration plus a constant deafening roar – that's what flying inside a Lancaster meant. Yet the Lancaster was a winner amongst the air crew. They trusted its massive wingspan and its four powerful Rolls Royce Merlin engines. It inspired confidence and gave them a feeling of security. It gave them no creature comforts whatsoever, and it brought them long noisy hours, yet the crews always had the faith that their Lancaster would get them there and back. That was all that mattered – that faith.

The Lancaster was the brainchild of Roy Chadwick, a brilliant and talented aircraft designer. Chadwick was a Lancashire lad, having been born in 1893 at Farnworth, a town lying to the north of the Mersey estuary. There was undoubtedly engineering "in the blood", for there were four generations of engineers in his family before him. In his late teens, Chadwick began working at the newly opened company of A. V. Roe (Avro) as personal assistant to Alliot Verdon-Roe, the pioneer aircraft constructor. Success followed success, as Chadwick's designs took shape in the form of popular aircraft, much heralded by the RAF. Until, that is, the less than felicitous Avro Manchester went into production.

The Manchester was a twin engined bomber, and it had problems. Big problems. The aircraft was designed with a powerful airframe enclosing a cavernous empty section that was the bomb bay. However, its engines (complex Rolls Royce Vultures) were not only unreliable, but they also didn't have the power needed for the airframe, causing (when lucky) loss of altitude and (when unlucky) complete engine failure and fire. Just over two hundred Manchesters were built – and more than half of them were lost because of engine failure.

It was touch and go. The Ministry of Aircraft was disillusioned with the performance of the Avro Manchester and serious consideration was given to going ahead with the rival Handley Page Halifax aircraft instead. But Chadwick's genius turned the situation round. Urban legend has it that the sketches for his new design were doodled on a copy of the *Manchester Evening News*. This new vision was to have a modified central section and crucially, bigger, extended wings with an immense span of over a hundred feet that would take four, instead of two, engines. And these were different engines, better engines – they were to be Rolls Royce Merlin engines.

The basic design of the Lancaster's airframe made it fairly easy to convert from a two engined assembly to a four engined version. When the production of the new aircraft soon began to outstrip the supply of Merlin engines, good fortune (in the shape of commercial co-operation from the other side of the Atlantic) stepped in to ensure that the new four engined Lancaster was in production fast. The Packard Motor Corporation of America undertook the licence manufacture of the engine and large numbers of Merlins were gratefully received at the Avro factories. The industrial organisation that was required to build the Lancaster was immense, involving thousands upon thousands of workers in two continents.

At the heart of the airframe of the mighty Lancaster was its robust central core in which there was a floor that ran the length of the section – and became, in fact, the roof of the bomb bay.

This not only added great strength to the aircraft, but it also made it very versatile, with a long and continuous, uninterrupted space that could be used for a variety of weaponry. The drawback to this, however, was that the main wing spars became major obstacles to movement within the aircraft, particularly for airmen wearing heavy clothing and flight boots. But comfort for the flight crew had to be sacrificed for the strength and versatility of the aircraft.

The Lancaster was a fine aircraft, a durable aircraft, that was fitted with four masterful engines, yet could easily fly on three, could manage on two and even (God willing) limp home on one. Its maximum speed was 270 miles per hour and it had a ceiling height of 22,000 feet – flying faster and higher than its precursor, the Manchester. Regarded as a pilot's aircraft, the Lancaster had speed, ceiling, and lifting power that no other aircraft of the day could match. Indeed, it was capable of taking off carrying a load equivalent to almost its own weight again – an astonishing achievement. The Lancaster established its superiority over other allied four engined bombers operating in Europe – a tribute to the genius of Roy Chadwick.

CHAPTER NINETEEN

Flying the Lancaster was a new experience for Chas, and the first few days at Skellingthorpe were spent on training flights (both by day, and crucially by night) with the Flight Commander. Night raids over enemy territory were the modus operandi of Bomber Command, while the United States Air Force flew most of the daytime raids in their Flying Fortresses. Just two days later, their first call came. The battle order notice was posted on the cork board in the Flight Office. The first operational flight for Chas, Duncan, Ginger, Ben, Ernie and their two new additions, Paddy Duggan and Nav Linton was to take place on the night of March 18. The notice gave no details and no destination – just names and the time of the briefing.

So how did they feel, these young men, about to fly their first op that might turn out to be their last? It was an accepted fact that unlucky novice "sprog" crews often didn't make it back to base owing to their lack of experience. A real Catch 22. Were they afraid? Not so much on their first mission, for they had yet to experience the full-blown horrors of a night sortie over enemy territory. That baptism of fire was yet to come. They were relieved to be finally through their years of hard training, and proud to be members of a numbered Squadron, a front line unit. There was an excitement too, a feeling of apprehension tinged with thrill. "An Awfully Big Adventure" as Peter Pan would have said. Anticipation too. Nervous yet controlled. Chas was the coolest of them all. His calmness was a great help to his crew, as it both motivated them and provided them with a feeling of security. He had a placid, stoic attitude that gave a determined feel to the uncertainty of their situation.

And why did they do it? What feelings inside motivated them to risk their lives, to leave their loved ones, to go into the unknown? Some grand and noble cause? Maybe. But more likely it was a desire to play their part, to "do their bit" just like everyone else. Patriotism certainly figured. King and Country, God and Harry! But it was much more than that. A deep seated and fundamental need to defend the home. To stand and be counted. To do what they believed was right.

And what of luck, what part did Lady Luck play? She was, of course, given every chance to play her part to the full. Lucky coins or maybe teddy bears, in fact all sorts of mascots and talismans were carried by the air crews hoping to cheat fate. For Duncan it was a silk scarf, given to him by Pauline that would hopefully steer him on a course of good fortune. Many of the air crew had similar lucky scarves, given them by their wives or girls.

The crews assembled in the Briefing Room at four in the afternoon; experienced men and young novice crews alike, all waiting with bated breath to receive instructions for their imminent flight over enemy territory. Everyone's eyes were on the curtained section at the front of the room, behind which lay the maps of the target area. Ginger glanced nervously across at Chas as they waited for the senior officers to arrive. Chas looked relaxed, but it took a conscious effort for him not to show the inner turmoil he was experiencing. He felt Ginger's gaze on him and with his characteristic, lop-sided, half smile on his face, turned towards him and silently mouthed the words "it'll be alright." Ginger smiled back and nodded. It would be alright. Chas would make sure of it. But the knot of fear deep in his belly wouldn't go away. Ginger watched as the officers, preceded by the Group Captain, entered the room and took their places. He held his breath as the Wing Commander began to speak.

"Gentlemen, the target for tonight is Frankfurt in the Rhine Valley, specifically the petro-chemical works and the iron and steel factories." There was an attentive silence in the room, all eyes focused on the charts and maps that the Wing Commander pointed to as he spoke. He continued to deliver the main information that the crews would need for the mission; the take-off time, the route they would follow and the altitude at which they would be flying. The Meteorological Officer then stepped forward and explained the likely weather conditions that might be encountered on the flight; finally the Intelligence Officer added further essential details that each crew needed to be aware of. The first briefing was over. The Wing Commander ended with a brisk

"Any questions? No? OK then, good luck, chaps – and don't do anything I wouldn't do!"

The crews filed out to go to their respective, separate briefings for further detailed information. Duncan joined the other wireless operators for the Signals briefing where they were given their codes, radio frequencies and other vital details. At the other separate briefings, maps were handed out to the navigators and bomb aimers, fuel and bomb load details were learned and much else besides. The men all mustered back again for their final crew session in the main briefing room and then it was off for their final meal – a slap-up "breakfast" whatever the time of day – of fried bacon and eggs.

The uncertainty was over, their imagination could stop playing tricks. They now knew what their first target would be: Frankfurt in the Rhine Valley. Eight hundred and forty six aircraft in total were to take part in the operation. Three quarters of them were Lancasters, the rest were Halifaxes, plus a small group of Mosquitos – the Pathfinders – who would fly ahead and mark the targets.

There was no time to dwell on "ifs" and "buts" – no time to think too deeply or worry if luck would be on their side. It was for real. It was now. Everything they had learned, everything they had yearned for, was right there before them. They could almost taste it.

The aircraft that would take part in the mission were almost ready. The ground crews had been working on them all day, checking and testing the engines, the instruments and the hydraulics. The armourers had loaded the bomb bays and fed the rounds of ammunition into the gunners' turrets. The oil and petrol dowsers were all filled up ready to transport the aviation fuel to the waiting Lancasters. The parachutes were checked and ready; the food rations and thermos flasks of hot tea were prepared. Now all that was needed was the air crew. They put on their flying suits and gathered up their maps, log books, parachutes and flasks and headed out to the Bedford trucks that would take them to the aircraft lined up at the dispersal points. Sitting inside the truck, many of the young men would smoke a cigarette or two, hoping against hope to calm their nerves. The ground crew were waiting, ready for the pre-flight inspection that the air crew would undertake with them. With a thoroughness that showed their lives depended on it, they inspected all essential parts of their aircraft, paying special attention to the bomb load and its security. The aircraft was ready: fuelled, armed, serviced and awaiting her crew.

Chas's Lancaster was one of twelve that would be leaving Skellingthorpe that evening. His young crew had all climbed up the access ladder and squeezed through the narrow fuselage, to reach their respective positions. It felt claustrophobic inside at first, and the main wing spars were high and had to be clambered over (not easy in full flying kit). But for the gunners there was an even trickier obstacle ahead. It was necessary for them to manoeuvre themselves into their turrets, as the space was very restricted. Ginger's rear gunner position ("Tail End Charlie") was possibly the most awkward and confined spot on the aircraft. Some tall rear gunners with big feet found it impossible to get into their turret with their footwear on, so they would put their flying boots in first, and then shuffle in after them and somehow get into their boots once they were installed in their post. The rear turret was accessed through the narrow tail space, and the gunner had to sit on the metal spar and then inch his way down in a sitting position, finally easing himself into the turret and then closing the two foot high doors that effectively shut him off from the rest of the aircraft. Ginger had a fairly small frame, so he was able to ease himself into the turret with his boots already on, but it was still a tight and very cramped location, stuck in a metal and Perspex blister at the very end of the aircraft. He felt vulnerable. And he was.

Both the rear and mid-upper gunners were equipped with electrically heated oversuits, boot liners and gauntlets, as the aircraft's rudimentary heating system didn't reach their turrets. Ernie's position in the mid-upper turret, suspended on a canvas sling seat with his lower body in the draughty fuselage and his head and shoulders in the plexiglass dome, was not one to be envied either. The gunners' workspaces were too small to store their parachutes in, so they had to leave them outside the turret. And pray they never needed to use them.

Duncan clambered over the high main spar and settled into his wireless operator's position, at the rear of the pilot, behind a bulk head wall. He put first his log book and then his code book on to the small table in front of the Marconi radio and breathed in slowly, settling into his seat. The space was cramped and there was just enough room to get his legs under the table beside the large radio batteries. He checked behind him to make sure that the bag of spares was stowed alright. He was something of a "Jack of all trades" like most wireless operators – as they could be called on to see to all the odds and ends, and fix little emergencies such as faulty doors and so on. Dunc felt in the bag for the familiar shapes of pliers and screwdriver, just to make sure the kit was there in case he needed it. He ran his hand along the Verey pistol, the flare that could be used in an emergency should they crash in friendly territory. And finally he mouthed a silent prayer.

Nav Linton clambered along the fuselage after Duncan and eased himself into his seat, just behind the pilot, facing the right side of the aircraft. His eyes were not yet fully accustomed to the semi darkness and he screwed them tight to hasten their adjustment. Opening them again, he glanced at his main instruments – the altimeter, airspeed indicator and compass – as he laid out the charts he would be working with to get them to Frankfurt. And back.

"Flaming hell Nav!" cursed Ben Lawrence, as he squeezed around Linton who was holding up one of the charts to reposition it on his desk top. Ben slapped Linton on the back good-naturedly and ruffled his hair, as he worked his way along to his crash position behind the wings. As bomb aimer, Ben would take up his position in the front turret at the nose of the Lancaster after take-off.

Chas settled himself into the pilot's seat on the left hand side of the cockpit. His high-backed seat had a bullet proof back, and was the only part of the Lancaster that had any armour protection. He manoeuvred his parachute pack underneath him to serve as a cushion, though it certainly didn't add much in the way of comfort. He ran his eyes over the control panel and noticed that the luminous paint that they were marked out with was just beginning to glow as the daylight started to fade. He adjusted his oxygen mask and glanced over at Paddy Duggan, his new flight engineer. He was a good man and proficient at his job, but Chas was a bit troubled by the fact that he couldn't always tell what Paddy was saying on account of his rich Irish brogue. Chas smiled to himself and wondered if maybe Paddy had problems understanding his own Australian accent. If he did, he hadn't shown it, or perhaps he was just being deferential to his skipper.

Paddy felt Chas's gaze on him and turned his head. The light was dimming fast and the cockpit had taken on an eerie glow.

"Nearly ready skipper".

"I'll check all positions now" replied Chas.

It was time. They were almost ready. Doubts, fears, apprehension and the more tangible physical feelings of sickness were pushed to the backs of their minds, as one by one, each member of the crew reported over the intercom that he was ready and that all equipment was in order. Chas signalled to the ground crew that he was ready to start the engines. The door was closed. There would be no turning back.

CHAPTER TWENTY

A startled blackbird, chattering indignantly, flew out of an old oak tree on the edge of the copse, as the first of the Lancaster's Merlin engines burst noisily into life. The grass around the edge of the hard standing was flattened as the huge propeller lashed the air. Coughing and spluttering, the second engine started up; the ground crew hooked up the booster battery to the third and then the fourth engine. Now all four Merlins were roaring with an intensity that made the airframe vibrate – their initial random lurching soon settling into a distinctive, rhythmic throb. The backdraft tossed the branches of the trees on the edge of the nearby copse as if they were in a gale. Inside, Paddy Duggan watched the gauges intently as Chas reported to the control tower that he was ready to taxi.

The ground crew pulled the wooden chocks from in front of the wheels and the huge aircraft slowly lurched forward. A roar from the outer starboard engine, countered by a brief burst of the opposite inner engine carefully turned the Lancaster out from its dispersal onto the perimeter track. Chas's hands remained firm and strong on the brake lever to hold the plane steady and stop it running away. There was no powered assistance, so brute force was often needed to control the massive aircraft as it inched forward to join the other eleven Lancasters for take off. The air in the Old Wood at Skellingthorpe shook as the roar of almost fifty massive Merlin engines reverberated together. They were lined up on the runway now. The on-lookers who had gathered nearby, stepped back so as not to be deafened by the roar. The ground crews and the women from the WAAF had turned out as they always did, to bid farewell and God speed to their friends.

Whispered prayers flew to heaven from silent lips. Please let them return.

Too busy to pray, yet bathed in the nerve-jangling tension of imminent take-off, the crew responded to Chas's last minute questions as he halted the aircraft at right-angles to the runway. A moment to pause, a relaxing breath, and a watchful eye on the airfield's Aldis lamp. Then came the steady green light that indicated the previous aircraft in the queue had taken off safely and was airborne. Chas put down the flaps for take-off, applied the brakes and revved the powerful engines hard until the Lancaster was straining to go. Slowly he released the brakes, feeling the immense force of the Merlins surging forward. Paddy had his hand underneath Chas's on the throttles to make sure they stayed fully open – losing power at this stage was not an option they wanted. They moved slowly, almost ponderously, at first, engines screaming. Then ever faster, bumping, rattling, speed increasing, faster, faster, faster still. Chas pushed the control column forward – the tail came up – take off speed was reached. The point of no return. Chas pulled back on the control column, Paddy took over the throttles and the massive, laden aircraft miraculously – majestically – soared into the air.

Over the Old Wood, over Stone's Place Fishpond and the Fosse Way, over the golden towers of the Cathedral, climbing ever upward, the Lancaster carried her crew. Long shadows darkened the Lincolnshire landscape that lay below them as they soared higher, to reach their cruising altitude. There they would circle, with the rest of their squadron from Skellingthorpe, waiting to join the rest of the massed bomber stream – the other hundreds upon hundreds of aircraft – that would all soon cross the east coast of England, some over the Fens and the Wash, some further north over the Humber.

"Hi Skip." Linton's soft Canadian accent crackled over the intercom to give Chas the course readings for their target.

"150 degrees magnetic, Skipper. Estimated time of arrival at rendezvous point 18.40 hours at 10,000ft."

"On course, Nav" confirmed Chas.

Cut off from the rest of the crew out in the remote Perspex tail blister, Ginger gazed out at the gentle velvet darkness that completely surrounded him. It almost felt as if he was floating. If it hadn't been for the roar of the engines and the vibrations that could be felt throughout the entire airframe, he could almost have convinced himself that he wasn't part of the aircraft at all.

He smiled to himself as he recalled a line from "Peter Pan" that his dear mother used to read to him many years ago.

"Second star to the right, and then straight on till morning" Ginger whispered to no-one at all.

CHAPTER TWENTY ONE

The dark skies over the North Sea had been the rendezvous for hundreds of aircraft from the different Squadrons – from there the bomber stream had set course for Frankfurt. While they were over Britain, the aircraft had had their navigation lights on, but once over the North Sea all lights were extinguished. The new crews who hadn't been on ops before usually took their places toward the back of the bomber stream. Chas had fallen in with the protocol, which meant that they were flying in the slipstreams of hundreds of aircraft – and it felt like riding a bumpy cart along a very rocky road. From time to time the sudden turbulence caused one or other of the Lancaster's wings to drop and they would lose a little height. When it happened, Chas pulled back on the control column hard so they could regain their position. Duncan wondered how Ernie McIlwaine was doing, up in his turret, in the rough conditions, as their previous long flight over France had given him such awful nausea. Chas had been thinking the same too, and his deep voice came over the crew's headphones.

"Ernie – how are you feeling?"

Ernie was grateful for the concern and put everyone's mind at rest by confirming that he wasn't feeling too bad. Just nervous. It was a difficult time, as they flew on, ever closer to enemy territory, ever closer to the massive anti-aircraft batteries along the Dutch coast. It was rumoured that some "chicken" crews dumped their bomb loads in the sea, then circled round for a few hours before returning back to base – but they were usually found out, and the shame was unbearable. Chas's distracting words of concern, reassuring and calming, gave his crew the confidence they needed to stay composed, as they drew ever nearer to the waiting guns. It wasn't only the anti-aircraft defences they had to worry about, there were also *Luftwaffe* night fighter squadrons based in Holland. Ernie and Ginger needed to stay on full alert, scanning the surrounding skies for danger. Chas checked with his gunners over the intercom to make sure that they were vigilant and watchful.

"Eyes peeled here, Skip" chimed in Ginger.

"All quiet on the Western Front for now" said Ernie, with a relieved smile.

No sooner had the words left the gunners' lips, than a massive cluster of bright red flashes erupted in the air around the aircraft. The acrid smell of cordite permeated the Lancaster and the muffled "krumpp" of exploding flak could be heard above the screaming Merlins. Tiny metal fragments from the burst shells nearby hit the aircraft's fuselage like scattered hailstones on a tin roof. It startled and shocked them all. They'd experienced flak on their leaflet run to Orleans, but although it had felt close at the time, it hadn't been as close a call as this. And they weren't through it yet. More red and now yellow flashes too, but closer to the ground. A sliver of moonlight gave Ben a view below the aircraft of dense clouds of smoke. Then suddenly they were through it. The only sound was the distinctive throb of the four Merlin engines, carrying them forward toward their target.

As the flak died away, Duncan concentrated intently on the "Monica" equipment. He'd studied hard at Swinderby for a moment such as this. He was acutely aware that they might be stalked by fighters – twin-engined *Messerchmitts* or perhaps *Junkers* 88s- and that their favoured approach would be to come at the Lancaster from below and behind. The two gunners were also on edge, their eyes were everywhere, scouring the darkness for predators. A chandelier flare in the black skies behind them startled Ginger and he released a brief burst of machine-gun fire into nothingness. The flare hung in the sky, illuminating everything for miles around, then slowly faded. Still Duncan watched his "Monica" screen.

Then he saw it. A blip on the screen. Or was it? Could his mind be playing tricks on him in the semi-darkness? There it was again, closer this time. No doubt about it, they were being stalked and their would-be attacker was closing fast. The fighter's *modus operandi* was well known as *Schrage Musik*. Jazz Music. A dance of death. The fighter would shimmy in from behind, keeping in step with the bomber while hiding in its blindspot, below its soft, unprotected underbelly. Then the fighter would shoot a slanting salvo directly into the unwary bomber's fuel tanks and side-step quickly away before all hell was let loose, leaving the Lord of the Dance to take His own.

Another method of striking was to aim right at the back of the bomber. The first surprise burst of fire would take out the exposed tail gunner, allowing the rest of the aircraft to be attacked almost at leisure. Neither of these events was going to happen if Duncan had any say in the matter. His reactions were fast.

"Skip. Wireless Operator here. Enemy aircraft approaching on our port side from behind."

Voicing a gasp of shock, Ginger excitedly confirmed the sighting. Chas didn't waste a moment. With lightning reflexes, his strong hands on the controls, he began to weave the heavy aircraft from side to side. A moving target wasn't an easy one, hopefully the fighter would leave them alone and go off in search of easier pickings. Duncan held his breath and tried to focus on the "fishpond" radar screen as the aircraft lurched crazily, momentarily disorienting him. Over the intercom came a small, stifled and nauseous groan from Ernie in the upper turret.

Duncan stared, there was no doubt about it, the blip was further away and off to port. Another cycle and it was further still.

"Skipper, we're losing him. You've done it".

Duncan's words washed relief over his fellow crew members. Chas allowed his shoulders to relax a little, stretching his chin upward to release some of the strain.

"Good show lads. Gunners, keep your eyes peeled and Dunc, keep watching that radar". Chas praised them while also keeping them alert and warning them not to drop their guard for even one moment. But they weren't about to. Every man was on edge, praying, hoping and watching. Ever watching.

A sudden blast of icy air and a massive roar from the rear of the fuselage made Duncan's stomach churn. The navigator and engineer had heard it too and several shocked expletives chorused over the intercom. Duncan picked up his portable oxygen cylinder and, breathing hard, struggled to make his way toward the back of the narrow plane to find out what had happened. Climbing over the bulky main spar in the cramped fuselage, in full flying kit plus an oxygen cylinder, was not easy. He bashed his shin on the hard metal and bit back a yell. As he neared the rear of the Lancaster, the deafening roar became a scream and freezing air assaulted his flesh. Then he saw the cause of the problem. The rear door had blown open, possibly during the erratic weaving they'd done to lose the fighter. He'd have to close it. The very thought made him sick with fear, but there was no time to dwell on the awfulness of the situation, he simply had to get the door closed. He fought his way back to his wireless operator's station and explained the problem over the intercom, adding an un-necessary plea to Chas to keep the aircraft steady while he attempted to close the door.

Despite the intense cold from the freezing air streaming in through the open gap, Duncan could feel the sweat pouring down his back as he made his way to the rear of the plane, hanging on to the metal struts when possible. He'd strapped on his parachute quickly, just in case, but he tried not to think of what might happen if he fell out. It was one thing practising jumping off an eight foot high bit of scaffolding during training, but it was an entirely new state of affairs to be stood in front of an open aircraft door when you're flying at 20,000 feet. Battling against the rush of air coming in through the doorway, he forced his way to the open chasm. It was impossible to breathe. His oxygen cylinder seemed to be empty and it was a weight that he didn't need. He dumped it on the ground and wedged it as best as he could. Now the door. He had to inch past the gaping chasm to get hold of it, but the massive force of the inrushing air had forced it flat against the inner wall of the fuselage. Duncan got his shoulder behind it and pushed with his entire weight toward the void. It was like battling against twenty men. Adrenalin rushed through his blood, he grunted and strained. A face – it was Pauline's – somehow flashed into his mind and whispered "You can do it". He strained again and suddenly the roaring stopped. The door was closed. Quickly, gasping for breath in the rarefied atmosphere, Duncan fixed the catches shut. Lurching forward, he grabbed the empty oxygen cylinder and staggered back down the fuselage.

"I closed it, Skip" Duncan gasped into the intercom, as he regained his seat and grabbed for his oxygen mask. His chest felt as if it was about to burst as he gulped in air. Relaxing a little, he faintly heard Chas's words of praise before they were drowned out by a chorus of cheers from the rest of the crew.

"Piece of cake" teased Ben. Duncan just smiled to himself.

But the pressure didn't ease off. The light-hearted respite that Duncan's victory with the door had given them, was short lived. As they neared the target area, tension rose once more. At least the weather was on their side, for a patchy cloud cover had built up, affording the bombers a little protection from the waiting searchlights, guns and fighters below.

Reality differs markedly from the text book. You can read and learn, discuss and plan. You can study charts, and endure practical demonstrations and dummy runs until you are sure, so sure, that you know all you need to know. But nothing can prepare you for the reality of it. As the Lancaster droned on toward the target area, the crew prepared themselves for things unknown. Ahead, in the distance, they saw an endless maze of search lights criss-crossing the skies. Without warning, a massive burst of light exploded in the middle distance, ahead of the Lancaster, casting an unearthly glow on the surrounding cloud tops and briefly illuminating the cockpit. A flare? Another Lancaster caught by an enemy fighter? Chas told himself to think about it later. They had work to do.

"Bomb aimer, let's get the Window out now".

"Right Skip".

Ben picked up the first of the long, thin brown paper packages full of aluminium foil strips called Window that were designed to give false echoes on the enemy's radar screens. He had to push the packs, one bundle at a time, through the hatch in the floor of the aircraft's nose at the rate of one per minute. As they fell, they would burst open in the Lancaster's slipstream and scatter wildly. Ben was looking forward to getting rid of the packs as they cluttered up his already confined, working space. He untied the string that wrapped the first pack and pushed the package out: slowly and methodically the others followed, fluttering and then scattering in the night air. Ben then settled as comfortably as possible into the position required to direct the bomb drop, propping himself on his elbows, lying flat and face down, in the bomb aimer's nose. The bombsight was right in front of him –

his view was directly down to the ground. Not a position for anyone with vertigo.

By his side was the Mark 14, a large black "box of tricks" (strictly speaking, an early computer) into which information on the Lancaster's altitude, speed and course were fed, as well as other essential data. Using this information, an illuminated cross was projected onto the bomb-sight; Ben had to line up the target with the centre of the cross. He was a stickler for accuracy, and he was determined – so determined – to get it right. As he looked out, he saw a maze of search lights. Beams of high intensity luminescence intent on capturing an incoming bomber like a startled rabbit; hoping to hold the stricken aircraft in the brilliance long enough for the flak guns to home in on the "kill" before moving swiftly to the next victim.

The Lancaster was almost on the target. Ahead Ben could see the area marked out by the green and red coloured target indicators that had been dropped by the advance Pathfinders. Below the criss-crossed maze of searchlights and flak that tore apart the night skies, the ground seemed to be ablaze, a fury of seething colour. There were long fingers of red spreading ever wider, punctuated by flashes of intense and blinding white.

"Nearly there, Skipper" came Ben's steady voice, low and resolute. "Left, left. Steady. Right a bit, steady. Bomb doors open."

"Bomb doors open" confirmed Chas, holding the aircraft straight and level. The rest of the crew held their breath, knowing that they couldn't take any evasive action, should it be needed, and they were consequently helpless against any attack on themselves for the next few minutes.

The Lancaster surged upwards almost a hundred feet as the massive weight of its load shot out of the bomb bay and plunged to earth.

"Bombs gone" called Ben.

"Holding steady" Chas gripped the controls and confirmed his intention, as Ben prepared to take the requisite aiming point photographs that would show they had fulfilled their mission (without them the flight might not count towards the thirty they would need to complete a single tour of duty). Their flashes barely pricked the night.

"Photographs taken, thanks Skip" Ben relaxed for the first time in many hours. He realised that his left leg was in cramp, no doubt a combination of the awkward position he had got himself into, and the stress of his first operation. He went to rub it, but his attention was torn back to the vivid view of hell below.

Then, slowly the Lancaster banked and set a westerly course for home.

CHAPTER TWENTY TWO

They had all been exhausted when they got back to Skellingthorpe. The brief respite that had been felt once they had left the target area had been short-lived – their relief was misplaced. Night fighters and yet more deadly flak accompanied them, and they had still to run the gauntlet of the dreaded defences near the North Sea coast. Nerves jangling, eyes sore and stinging, limbs aching; each man felt an overwhelming relief when finally they had passed through the danger zones and the longed-for Dutch coast was sighted. Once across it, they could hope for a quieter passage on the final leg of their mission.

White lights, their brilliance piercing the pre-dawn darkness, marked out the runway at Skellingthorpe as Chas brought his Lancaster in to land. The plane's wheels touched down, bumped back up, then settled down once more into a juddering rhythm across the concrete, as the aircraft strained to brake. Finally it shuddered to a slow crawl and was taxied to its dispersal point on the perimeter. At last the crew could relax a little, though not for long, as they must endure a full briefing session before they could have their longed for breakfast of bacon and eggs.

Their profound relief at returning safely back home was short-lived, as just four nights later they were on their way back to Frankfurt again. They were given a different route to the target; to the north of the Dutch Zuider Zee which suited all the crews involved as it avoided both the worst of the flak and the dreaded night fighters. Just two days later, however, their orders came in again, Chas and his crew were to target Berlin, along with over 800 other aircraft from Bomber Command. Their Lancaster for the mission would be H-How, the same aircraft that had brought them safely back from Frankfurt.

Berlin, known to most aircrew as the Big City, was a formidable target that was both fiercely and ingeniously protected by a combination of menacing methods of attack (the night fighters plus of course the flak guns) and novel attempts at distraction. Several dummy towns had been built in which the recognisable open civic spaces as well as several major landmarks had been carefully replicated. Decoy target markers were used to try and entice the bombers away from the actual city, while the real buildings and open spaces in Berlin itself were camouflaged wherever possible. Enormous wooden bonfires were lit on many of the dummy sites to simulate burning buildings, and suggest direct hits on target had occurred. The same intense patriotism that was behind the defence of London and other major British cities was fully matched by the Berliners.

The raid on the night of March 24th was to be the last onslaught of a four month long campaign against the city in which Bomber Command had lost many aircraft and many men. By the end of that long March night, those losses grew to over one thousand aircraft plus thousand upon thousands of young lives, all in less than twenty weeks. The crews who set off that night knew they were risking their lives again, but unquestioningly they went through the now familiar routine of briefing, kitting up, taking off and then the long and dangerous haul in the dark of night; not knowing if they would return, not knowing what horrors, what pain, what unmentionable awfulness lay ahead. They clambered off the lorries at their dispersal points, ready and willing, representing a strange combination of Defenders of the Realm, Warriors of Destruction and Lambs to the Slaughter. Young men, determined to do their duty for King and Country, ready to lay down their lives in the cause of freedom.

Many of them would pay the ultimate sacrifice on that fateful March night.

The pilots had done the last minute checks with their crews, making sure they all had their essential kit and were carrying nothing that might cause them problems if they had to bale out over enemy territory. Pockets were emptied out and checked to make sure no one had forgotten a bus ticket or any British money. Nothing that could identify them or give away possibly useful information was to be carried. If captured, the only details they were to give were their name, rank and number. Rudimentary orienteering would be courtesy of a silk handkerchief on which was a printed map of France, Belgium and Holland. To gauge direction, all crew members had a pencil with a small compass on the end of it. Every man carried French and Dutch money plus a small passport photo (the latter could be used to make a fake passport by the Resistance, should circumstances arise). They all had a thermos flask of hot tea and some rations such as an apple, a bit of chocolate and maybe a biscuit or two. As extras there were usually some barley sugar sweets and a wakey-wakey tablet (the euphemism for Benzedrine) that was designed to keep eyes wide open and brains functioning at three in the morning. Their instructions, written orders, codes and anything secret was written on "flimsies" – which could be chewed and swallowed if capture was threatened.

They were ready. The weather wasn't too good in England but the forecasts for the route out and the target area itself were fair, though there was a warning that Berlin may have cloud cover and there could be a fairly strong north-westerly headwind for the return journey. Meteorology was in its infancy, with few means at the disposal of the forecasters with which to predict the crucial information needed by the aircrew for their long missions into the heart of Europe. Mosquitos or Spitfires would fly reconnaissance missions in broad daylight over Germany to gather vital information on air temperature and barometric pressure. They could easily be picked up by radar and were soft targets, as they had no defensive armour and no guns. The bravery of their crews, and those of the Coastal Command Halifaxes who flew out into the Atlantic in all weathers to gather similar data, is often overlooked. But that night, despite all efforts to garner as much information as possible in advance of the operation, they could not have hoped to have known about such a fickle phenomenon as the jet stream. Nobody could have known that the predicted, fairly strong wind would turn out to be a ferocious blast of doom.

The crews mustered, the aircraft took off and the bomber stream congregated over the North Sea. But a massive force is hard to hide, and as over eight hundred heavy bombers crossed Denmark, the warning drums began to beat. A decoy bomber group over France was dismissed with a blink of the eye. The main bomber stream was being watched and its target rapidly became clear. Soon Berlin – and more importantly, the *Luftwaffe* night fighters and the hundreds of flak guns and searchlight batteries – would be ready for the attack.

Ben Lawrence, peering down from his bomb aimer's bubble, could see the Big City aglow from many miles away. The Pathfinders had illuminated the target with their deep red indicator markers. The depth and intensity of the ruby colour was very distinctive – a testament to the quality of the British firework manufacturers whose skills were gratefully relied upon. A fair amount of cloud also covered the area, Ben could see their layered tops from his vantage point. "Wanganui" sky markers had been used to show the parts of the target area that were obscured by cloud, and the intense red glow from these flares was illuminated further by the yellow stars that flashed out from the Pathfinders' pyrotechnics.

Chas was looking too, as was Ernie McIlwaine in his mid upper gunner's turret. Not a word was spoken as they stared out into the maelstrom of light that lay ahead. The ground was ablaze. The sky was alight. It was essential, vital, to hold their nerve and not drop their load too early. They must fly on, into the jaws of the hell that lay ahead. There was tracer fire right ahead and searchlight beams sliced the sky. Still they flew on, bumping and jolting in the tangled, invisible grid of slip streams as eight hundred aircraft attempted to fly over the target in just fifteen minutes.

"Bombs gone".

H-How surged upward as the massive weight was released. Chas held the huge Lancaster as steady as he could, but the fierce winds were proving to be a significant and unanticipated problem. As Chas set course for their return journey from Berlin to the North Sea coast, the speed of the winds in the jet stream increased to almost hurricane force, slowing down the aircraft considerably.

Mother Nature was about to deal an especially nasty blow.

The majority of the returning aircraft were blown south, to an area they would have hoped (with every fibre of their being) to have avoided – the Ruhr – the area that was ironically known as "Happy Valley" by more experienced air crew who had had bitter experience of the intense, defensive anti aircraft activity there (and their subsequent chances of being hit or shot down). Heavily defended, armed to the teeth with searchlights, flak guns and fighters, the Ruhr was the nightmare that the airborne survivors of the raid were blown right into. To make matters worse, their airspeed dropped as the force of the oncoming wind increased, making them easier targets. They were being blown into dangerous skies. Sacrificial skies.

The records indicate that many flak batteries were able to score successes. In human terms these euphemistic words serve to indicate that many aircraft, struggling home, carrying brave young men, were violently blasted out of the skies. And what of the people who operated those guns, in defence of their country? Or flew the fighters that so successfully attacked the lumbering bombers? In other times, under different circumstances, these men might have all shaken hands and been friends with their enemies. They were alike in so many ways. Young, patriotic, devoted, determined and brave. Circumstances pitched them against each other. Another time, another day, another world away and they would have shared a drink, and laughed and joked together. But not that day.

H-How flew on, through the nightmare that was the Ruhr, its four Merlin engines roaring, eating up fuel, their exhaust ports spewing out rivers of crimson flame, barely hidden beneath their baffle covers. Fighting hard against the monstrous wind, the aircraft clawed its way toward the North Sea, ever homeward, ever closer to safety.

It was bitterly cold, Duncan hoped that his hands wouldn't freeze up totally. He'd heard of one wireless operator who ended up using his elbows to tap out morse messages because his hands were frozen. But they didn't have too far to go now, and visions of crisp bacon and luscious eggs for breakfast danced before his tired eyes. His reverie was interrupted by Chas's urgent voice over the intercom.

"Wireless Op, send a message back to base, prefixed P. The engineer and I have calculated that we're low on fuel, must be because we're flying hard into the wind and we went off course getting out of the flak in "Happy Valley". I don't think we're going to make it back to Skellingthorpe".

Chas's words sent a chill through the rest of the crew. While Duncan immediately set about sending his message with its prefix P indicating that the aircraft was in trouble, the others considered their plight. Ginger, isolated in the rear turret, stared out at the churning dark void below that was the North Sea. Ditching into the freezing waters in the black night was his worst fear. He remembered the training exercises they'd done in the swimming baths at Turweston. His inability to swim had made him a liability and it was only with Duncan's help that he'd got into the dinghy that had bobbed gently on the surface of the swimming pool. The thought of their aircraft having to put down onto the open sea, even possibly breaking up on impact, filled him with an immense and terrible dread. Despite the warmth trickling through his heated suit, he felt himself turn icy cold with fear, and his lips began to mouth a silent prayer. He knew he wouldn't make it if they ditched, but his faith in Chas was strong.

"Please God, give Chas the strength to get us home" he whispered to the clouds.

His faith in Chas was not misplaced. The pilot took the Lancaster down to a lower altitude where the winds seemed less fierce and the aircraft wasn't fighting so hard to make headway. They'd been given clearance to land at the United States Airforce base at Raydon in Suffolk, near the little village of Hadleigh just west of Ipswich. Raydon was in the heart of Gainsborough country, famous for its flat pastures and gentle streams, but more importantly for H-How it was home to the USAF 357th, 358th and 353rd Fighter Groups, and it was just a few minutes flying time from the North Sea coast near Felixstowe. The Lancaster limped the final few miles, losing height rapidly, as the estuaries of the Stour and Orwell came into view in the first glimmers of dawn. Ginger breathed an audible sigh of relief as the Lancaster's wheels touched down on the long concrete runway.

For the following eight hours or so, Chas and his crew enjoyed a taste of America – and what a sweet taste it was. The USA wasn't under strict rationing like Britain, and so the USAF air bases had a wide choice of tasty food on offer. The bacon and eggs that Duncan had been salivating over in anticipation just a few hours earlier were replaced that chill March morning by fried spam, eggs and delicious hash browns – crisped to brown perfection on the outside and succulently moist within. Nectar. The Yanks treated their buddies well. After giving them time for a short nap they then plied them with real coffee and Hershey's chocolates. It was a welcome interlude in a time of great stress. H-How was given the "once-over" by the USAF engineers, and after being filled up with aviation fuel, Chas and his crew set off for their base – back to Skellingthorpe.

In the "night of the strong winds" the RAF crews had fought the weather as well as the enemy. They suffered at the hands of both. Seventy two aircraft, each carrying a seven man crew failed to return home. At the bases, those who had arrived back noticed that some of their fellow crews were missing. But no one questioned orders to fly again the next day. They went on, despite losses, despite seeing friends go missing and aircraft shot down. Day after day. The same routine; the briefing, getting dressed up ready, taking off, and then the long haul to the target.

Then if they were lucky, the long haul back again. Lady Luck was a fickle friend.

CHAPTER TWENTY THREE

Fog – dense and damp – settled on large areas of eastern England during the last days of March. Early spring is a capricious time. One day might be gentle and mild, with the first signs of swelling green buds and a zephyr of warmth in the air. The very next day could bring cold winds or worse, the thick and clammy fogs that smothered the unwary in a blind blanket of bone-chilling dampness. The murk spread from the countryside to the towns where it became smog; polluted with smoke and grime. Bomber Command grounded all its aircraft – giving the airmen a brief and chilly respite.

On the 29th all crews were alerted to the possibility of an op and the aircraft were prepared and made ready. Late in the day the mission was cancelled and the crews were stood down – but not for long. Thursday the 30th dawned bright and cold with no sign of the recent fogs. The crews knew before ten in the morning that there was to be a major op that night, but with the moon still half full and bright many of them believed it would surely be cancelled. Most aircraft were already prepared from the aborted mission the previous day, so when word went out that the bomb loads already on the aircraft were to be lessened to allow more aviation fuel to be taken on, the new buzz was that a long trip was on the cards. It had to be somewhere very deep in the heart of Europe – and as it was clear that this was going to be a big one, plenty of amateur prophets of doom found their voices. After a short pre-briefing, the aircrews filled up on their bacon and eggs, despite jaded appetites. The thought on many minds, as they ate their last forkful of streaky bacon, was that it might be their very last. Most of them had worked out what the survival rate was, and they were all aware the odds were not on their side. Roughly half of all aircrew were lost before they had even completed ten missions. Were they about to embark on a one way trip with no return ticket? And what was their destination?

The answer was soon revealed at the full briefing. The target was to be Nuremberg. There was a hush at the revelation. Nuremberg was an industrial and transportation hub, filled with railway yards and sidings, packed with tanks and armoured vehicles. But it had a further significance, an emotional and symbolic significance, for Nuremberg was the birthplace of the Third *Reich* and the scene of the infamous *Nazi* Rallies. There was silence in the briefing room as the news sank in, and the intended route that the bomber stream would fly that night, was explained. They would be taking a long and direct path deep into enemy territory, flying close to the heavily defended areas around Frankfurt and the Ruhr. Then there would be a turn to the south and a short, unexpected approach to Nuremberg, followed by a direct route back home – or so they hoped. The notoriety of the area they would be flying so close to, was well known to all in the room. The bantering words of a familiar spoofed song that was sung to the tune of the "Quarter Masters Store" came into several minds.

There was flak, flak, bags of bloody flak. In the Ruhr, in the Ruhr, There was flak, flak, bags of bloody flak. In the valley of the Ruhr.

Wry smiles were exchanged and a few "devil-may-care" shoulders were shrugged, but most were only too aware that this route posed a risk.

The Commanding Officer at Skellingthorpe had a habit of closing his briefing sessions by asking one of the newest aircrew to repeat the salient points of the instructions. On the night of March 30th 1944, his gaze fell on a sprog gunner and he requested that the young airman should come to the front of the room and run through the main elements of the forthcoming mission. The victim, a young sergeant, with nerves jangling and palms sweating, stood up and stammered his inadequate response. The lad had made a complete hash of it, his memory throwing up flashbacks of similar embarrassing moments at school and the resultant sharp sting of ruler on flesh. But the mortifying feeling he had that afternoon as he garbled his response was far worse than any physical slap. He not only had embarrassed himself, but he had also embarrassed his pilot. At the time, he had wanted the ground to swallow him up. As it happened, his wish was granted some hours later, when the aircraft he was flying in was shot by the cannons of a night fighter over the Ruhr and the burning remains of his Lancaster buried themselves into Mother Earth below. But that was to come.

The day remained chilly and bright, though there were some light showers of sleet mixed with snow. The clear weather and in particular, the knowledge that there would be a half moon that night, continued to weigh on the minds of many crews. They'd been told that the "met" reports had predicted high cloud that would mask the moon, but the worries remained. Exhaustion coupled with unease caused tension in many RAF airfields that day. It was going to be a very long op. The flying time for a return mission to Nuremberg was around eight hours, in cramped and extremely uncomfortable conditions. Most of the men had been to Frankfurt twice, to Berlin and to Essen all within the previous eight days. They were worn out and they were edgy. As day turned into dusk, and darkness descended upon the land, many glanced up at the silver moon shining brightly and crossed their fingers.

At Skellingthorpe Chas and his crew were due to fly their favourite Lancaster, H-How. It was their one good omen on a day that seemed full of foreboding. Everyone felt uncomfortable after the briefing, especially when the sprog gunner had made such a hash of repeating the instructions for the op. And everyone was unhappy about the moon. Much attention was being paid to lucky talismans and superstitious routines, such as the final serendipitous act of urinating on the tail wheel of the Lancaster. Through this strange routine it was hoped that Destiny would be on their side. Duncan fingered his lucky neckerchief – the silk scarf Pauline had given him. He'd started to write on it, carefully scripting the names of the towns that he had flown to on missions. Frankfurt, Berlin and Essen – the names stood out in stark, black ink on the once pristine whiteness of the filmy fabric. Would he be back in the Nissen hut at Skellingthorpe tomorrow to pick up his fountain pen and add "Nuremberg" to the list? He prayed it would be so as his lips silently mouthed his wife's name "Pauline".

In the darkness of night, H-How taxied out of the dispersal and took its place on the perimeter track near the end of the queue. The green Aldis light flashed and the first of nineteen Lancasters roared down the runway. The moonlight glinted on its dark grey fuselage and illuminated the little crowd of well wishers on the ground; waving, praying and whispering "God speed". H-How was number fourteen in the queue. They lumbered slowly forward watching, engines growling, waiting, as the green light came on and it was their turn. Faster, the airframe rattling and straining, the noise of the massive Merlins deafening. Ninety eight, ninety nine, one hundred, one hundred and one, one hundred and two, one hundred and three, one hundred and four, one hundred and five miles an hour. At that the wheels broke contact with the ground and the aircraft surged upwards defying gravity, defying logic, carrying its massive load of fuel and high explosives – and seven men. Seven hearts beating a mantra that invoked hope. An eighth heart, a silent and unwanted crewman named "Fear" flew with them; unseen but known, yet only rarely acknowledged. Tonight he would stay close by their sides.

Behind them the next aircraft made ready to leave. As it approached the point of no return, a tyre burst throwing the plane into a massive sideways skid. The pilot, a fellow Australian and a friend of Chas, felt the controls shudder and jolt as his Lancaster thundered along, slewing off the runway. He struggled to regain control as the aircraft, engines screaming, tipped sideways, gouging deep scars along the ground and tearing off part of a wing and one of its massive engines. The crew were shaken and bruised, and the mid upper gunner mildly concussed, but as they staggered off their broken aircraft each man looked up at the lambent moon and thanked his lucky stars.

High above in the dark velvet skies, Chas banked H-How, heading out towards the Wash and the assembly point for the bomber stream. A light northerly tail wind was forecast that would speed them on their way, and their course was set to follow the line of the predicted high cloud. The moon would be low and hopefully fully set by the time they were on their way back. At least that was how it was supposed to be.

The bomber stream formed easily. The night was bright and clear as a bell with just a few wisps in the sky to remind them of the cloud cover they so desperately needed. With the Pathfinder force at its head, a swarm of around eight hundred aircraft almost seventy miles in length formed over the North Sea and headed towards the Belgian coast. Ironically, the navigation and radar equipment that the RAF crews were using and depending on, unwittingly became a "spy in the camp". Unbeknown to Bomber

Command, many hundreds of miles away, the German radio monitoring service was paying close attention to the massed electronic signals its listening posts were picking up. Already they knew from the sheer volume and timing that a major raid was imminent. And they were ready for it.

As the stream crossed the Belgian coast near Knokke there was light flak that bothered hardly anyone. The few wraiths of cloud vanished and the moon shone ever brighter as the bombers continued over Belgium; high above the Meuse, past Liege and onward. The northerly winds began to blow some of the aircraft into a slight drift and the bomber stream grew increasingly ragged. As the massed Lancasters and Halifaxes started to move over Germany heading for the Rhine Valley and that narrow gap between Bonn and Koblenz, the first night fighters appeared on the scene. At just after midnight, the witching hour, the carnage was about to begin.

The pilots of the *Messerschmitts* and *Junkers* fighter aircraft couldn't believe their luck. They'd looked out at the bright skies and were amazed that the allied attack hadn't been called off. They were brothers under the skin to the RAF crews – all were young men who wanted to protect their respective homelands. A shared desire to fly linked them and at times they would hold a reciprocal yet grudging respect for their adversaries. But any secret approbation had to be pushed to the back of their minds that night, for each and every man had a job to do and a patriotic duty to carry it out.

Against the clear dark sky, the aircraft of Bomber Command were starkly visible. The brilliant moonlight skipped and danced along their massive frames as they lumbered through the air. To add to Mother Nature's mischief, incandescent vapour trails began to appear in the atmosphere behind the bombers. They marked the aircraft out, like malevolent fingers pointing toward their prey. The *Luftwaffe* fighter pilots had an easy task – their quarry was both visible and vulnerable. They moved in for the kill.

The first Lancaster to be hit glowed gold, then scarlet, plunging downward belching black smoke. The next appeared to be rent apart in the skies, a vivid blood-red explosion scarred the air. Two Pathfinders were hit by cannon fire from fighters just below them – the pyrotechnic display caused by their exploding target indicators lit the skies for miles around. An arena of death, four miles up in the air, awaited the next victim. And on they came, heading into the terrible conflagration where immolation, and a terrible and awful end awaited so many.

The silver moonlight cast its traitorous glow on the scene. In a cruel twist of fate it not only gave the *Luftwaffe* fighters the visibility they desired for attack, but it also allowed the aircrew of Bomber Command to witness the appalling carnage and destruction of their compatriots. From the cockpit, the astrodome, the gunners' and the bomb aimer's turrets, the view was the same. Everywhere they looked, aircraft were ablaze and parachutes were unfurling, often burning. Tracer fire, glowing balls of flame and massive explosions, furious and fearsome, clawed at the air. Ben Lawrence looked down from his bomb aimer's position and saw a blazing Lancaster flying straight ahead but losing height, sinking ever downwards as exploding bombs inside it erupted. It flew on and on, lower and lower, until eventually it hit the ground with a tremendous eruption of crimson flame. Ben closed his eyes and mouthed a silent prayer, thinking of the families of the doomed men, thinking too, of his own wife. The emotional shock chilled him to the bone.

Chas weighed things up fast. Though they were supposed to stay with the bomber stream (and usually it was a case of safety in numbers) he felt that they would stand a better chance of getting out of the surrounding slaughter by flying a little higher or getting out of the main group. The load they were carrying was huge, so gaining height wasn't much of an option. Chas banked the Lancaster and turned away from the main stream, while staying as close to the set course as possible. They were nearing their turning point, and a new southerly route, directly to Nuremberg, would be employed. Hopefully he could keep H-How out of the way of the fighters. They flew on, skirting the Ruhr, afraid and shocked but absolutely determined.

Luck was on their side. In the game of Chance, Chas was dealt a good hand on behalf of H-How that night, despite Mother Nature having a further nasty trick up her sleeve. The longed-for cloud finally appeared, but it was below them, as they approached the target on the final leg. The bright moon above shone on the bombers, turning them into perfect silhouettes above the fine grey cloud below. The *Luftwaffe* fighters now found that as they gained height, they could easily spot the bombers below them and claim yet more victims, but H-How was not amongst them that night.

They approached the target. The crew had much to occupy their minds, everyone was focused. Duncan received a final broadcast on the transmitter which confirmed that zero hour was unchanged, and began to wind in his trailing aerial. Ben was throwing out the brown paper packs of Window as fast as he could. In the pauses between each pack he switched on the gyro in his bomb sight and activated the heaters on the cameras in the bomb bay. Ernie and Ginger scanned the skies intently watching for enemy aircraft. Chas held H-How straight and level. Stay cool. There was flak. Green and red sky markers in the distance to their right and on the ground too, where the cloud was broken up.

Nav Linton spoke quietly over the intercom. "I don't think we're over the right target yet".

Ben confirmed it. "You're right, Nav. Skipper, something's not quite as it should be. I can see some kind of glow further ahead. The timing's wrong too – I think we should carry on."

Linton added "Maintain a course of 175 degrees magnetic, Skip."

They flew on with gritted teeth, through more flak and searchlights. As Duncan maintained his vigil watching the Monica screen, he saw a fast moving object coming toward them and quickly alerted the rest of the crew. Ginger's startled response confirmed their fears – a *Junkers* 88 was behind them some distance away. As Chas prepared to take avoiding action, Ernie McIlwaine's relieved voice gave them all momentary respite.

"He's gone. He's passed us by. He's after some other poor blighter."

McIlwaine's words choked in his throat with horror as his dark gunner's turret was suddenly illuminated by a vivid red glow. The *Luftwaffe* fighter had found its prey. McIlwaine watched as a Lancaster flying several hundred feet above them, and around half a mile off to their side, rolled over in flames. It fell, spinning and dripping immense tongues of fire.

Nearby a Halifax, was coming in over the target too, when another *Junkers* 88 struck, its fateful *Schrage Musik* fire hitting the inner starboard engine of the bomber. Three crew including the pilot baled out and were captured, but the Halifax blew up at fifteen thousand feet while the rest of the crew were leaving the plane. One of the men who perished was young Chris Panton, a nineteen year old flight engineer from Lincolnshire who had hoped to be a pilot one day.

Many hopes died that night.

H-How flew on. A smattering of "Wanganui" – the distinctive green and red sky markers peppered with yellow stars – lay ahead. Surely that was the target? Poorly marked, but it had to be their target. They made their final run. Ben Lawrence, lying flat in his bomb aimer's bubble, lined up his bomb-sight by what remained of the coloured pyrotechnics of the sky markers. H-How dropped its load through the thick cloud cover and rose upward, as if on the wings of Pegasus.

"Let's get the hell out of here, Skip" muttered Ben, as Chas banked the Lancaster away from the glow toward the friendly darkness.

It was a long three hour slog back to safety. Plenty of time to relive over and over again the visions of horror that they had borne witness to. Plenty of time for vengeful night fighters to seek out yet more victims. Plenty of time to think about the next mission. And the next and the next. Time to think of family back home, of wives or girlfriends, of happier times in the past and please God, of times to come. H-How lost height and sought cover in the thick cloud. The moon set just before 2 am and the clear sky had given way to a dense layer of stratus. The silent words on many lips whispering "if only it had been there just a few hours earlier."

As the returning aircraft saw the coast of England, many of them had lost enough height for the crew to remove their oxygen masks and finally take a welcome drink of tea from their thermos flasks. Never had it tasted so good. Over Selsey Bill, then a northerly flight path and a course turn over Reading and then on to the airfields where the flare-paths would be lit up ready, illuminating the countryside for miles around. The relief was enormous, almost home. In they came, through the low cloud and sleet showers. But danger was never more than an angel's breath away. At Silverstone, a Halifax limping in with just three engines, on a wing and a prayer, failed to line up with the runway and clipped the top of some low buildings. It smashed sideways, careering wildly and somersaulted before exploding and killing all but the tail gunner. One more casualty to add to the record books. One more to add to the total that would prove to be Bomber Command's heaviest losses of the entire Second World War for just one, single night. A night in which almost six hundred young RAF men were killed. More in just that one night than were lost in the entire Battle of Britain.

Telegrams were sent out. Rooms were cleared of personal belongings. But memories live on. They will never die.

CHAPTER TWENTY FOUR

After Nuremberg, Duncan (in common with many air crew) was given seven days leave. It was like a dream come true. In the midst of the hell, the madness and the fear, there was to be a taste of heaven. Seven whole days. Enough time to get back to Manchester and see Pauline. Time to hold her in his arms and tell her how much he loved her. How much she meant to him. How he would never leave her, God willing.

He had felt privileged that he was able to get home in the seven day furlough – Chas, of course, could not get back to his family in that short time. He'd explained to Duncan that he had some family friends up in the Lake District though, and he planned to go and stay with them for a few days. Manchester was about half way between Lincolnshire and the Lakes, and Duncan had wondered if he might invite Chas to stop off *en route* and meet Pauline. They didn't have their own home, but he knew that Pauline's mother would make Chas welcome.

The blissful week with Pauline in Manchester had simply flown by. As he sat on the train returning to Skellingthorpe, Duncan pulled up his collar to keep the draught off his neck and remembered the journey he had made just a few days earlier. How happy he had been as he'd travelled ever closer to Pauline, ever closer to home. He could still see her soft features when he closed his eyes. He'd done that many times over the past few months – especially on the return flight from Nuremberg when he had also prayed and thanked God for getting them safely back.

It had been wonderful when Chas had called in on them, and Duncan had felt proud as he introduced his beautiful young wife to the pilot. They'd all had tea and talked for a while, and

Pauline's family had been most impressed with the tall Australian airman. Later, when Chas said his farewells, he had turned to Pauline and said earnestly to her:

"Don't worry Pauline, I'll keep Duncan safe".

She had looked across at Duncan, her eyes filled with tears, and had grasped his hand.

"Thank you" she'd murmured, in a voice barely above a whisper.

It had been hard for them all. Their joy at returning back to England safely was tempered by the knowledge that they would have to fly again very soon. At the end of his leave in Manchester Duncan had held Pauline in his arms, wishing the moment would never end. She in turn had clasped him tightly, as if to keep the warmth of his body trapped within her very being so she might get through the months ahead. She had looked at him and pleaded for re-assurance.

"You'll be alright, won't you Duncan?" she had whispered.

But he hadn't been able to answer. He couldn't bring himself to speak. His mind had filled with images of burning aircraft: balls of fire plunging to earth. All he could hear was the sound of muffled flak and the roaring Merlins. Pauline had looked closely into his brown eyes when she'd realised he was not answering her. It had taken a moment before he could return her gaze. When he eventually did, she had seen pools of darkness in them and the subdued panic of distant fear.

Now, as he sat in the railway carriage on his way back to RAF Skellingthorpe, all he could think of was her. How much she meant to him, how precious his time with her was, and how he couldn't bear to imagine what she might feel, would say, would undergo, if he were not to return. He was afraid for himself, of course, but his fear for her was agony to bear. He wanted to protect her. To promise that there would never be any sadness, any pain. But he knew that the only sure thing about their future was that it was uncertain.

Looking down the years from our viewpoint today, one can only wonder how those young men and women did it. How did those airmen cope with the knowledge that when they flew off into the darkness of the night, on a mission, there was a strong chance that they might never return? How did they live with the dreadful, awful realisation that their end – should it come at twenty thousand feet – would be agonising, terrifying and the very stuff of nightmares? How did they live with the fear? How did it feel to those poor souls who knew their final seconds were right there before their very eyes? Maybe an insight from some who survived by the strangest of lucky circumstances can give an inkling of how it felt – of the fear that turned to calm. One said that he put his hands together and prayed. Another seemed to live his whole life again in just a few seconds. Who knows? Who really knows?

And how was it for the "lucky" ones who did return? How did they cope with knowing that many of their friends hadn't survived? Back at base, seeing bedside cabinets cleared of personal possessions; friendly names and faces missing. Are you grateful for being spared – or guilty because of it? Or both? Then how do you carry on when aircraft are exploding and burning in the air all around you? Watching them plummet from the skies, hearing the silent screams of forfeit lives.

What part of your character allows you to go on? What strength of mind is needed? What truths, or perhaps what lies, do you need to believe? It will never be me, perhaps? Maybe it's a sense of fatalism that is required? A feeling that there is no other option, no other way. You just had to do it. A duty that must be performed. To do and maybe to die?

That night, after Duncan had returned to Skellingthorpe, Pauline went outside and stood for a while looking at the stars. Her eyes sought out the brightest one so that she could "wish upon a star" as she had done many times in the past months. It was always the same wish – bring Duncan home safe.

How can you think, how can you breathe, when you know that your love is in danger and far away. No news or satellite coverage, nor television pictures showing everyone back home what's going on. No mobile phones for contact. Just your own imagination, ready to play tricks, ready to imagine the worst, and yet never truly able to know what hell and what terror your loved one is going through.

How could you carry on? You simply had to believe.

CHAPTER TWENTY FIVE

Many lives had been lost during that last week in March, and those who survived had been given a grandstand view of the carnage. But there was no trauma therapy, no counselling and no incisive delving into the subconscious. Instead the crews were simply addressed by the Commanding Officer whose job it was to get their spirits back up. Although only a privileged few knew it at the time, the Combined Forces were just weeks away from D-Day and their planned incursion into northern France to liberate Europe. It was imperative that the massive and terrible losses of both men and aircraft in those last weeks of March did not hold things up. The immediate need was to pave the way for the D-Day invasion and weaken the defences in Occupied France, by attacking supply dumps, troop concentrations, marshalling yards and transportation targets. A special team had also been set up, charged with neutralising the enemy's coastal radar chain and listening posts. There was to be no softening, no let up and no pause. The momentum of attack had to be maintained, and it was imperative that air supremacy was achieved for it was the only way to bring the hostilities to their final end.

Early April saw many squadrons engaged in training operations as well as sorties over France to targets such as Tours, Juvisy and La Chapelle plus attacks on various sites along the entire Channel coast (so as to disguise the actual D-Day landing locations). Then, toward the end of the month, 50 Squadron had a long op to Brunswick. It was on a Saturday night – just the kind of night when they should have been out with their girls, dancing the jitterbug to a Glenn Miller tune. After the debriefing on Sunday they all tried to catch up with much needed sleep.

Monday morning dawned brightly and the sun's golden rays penetrated the gloom of the dank Nissen hut, waking Duncan earlier than he would have liked. He blinked and rasped out a cough. His shoulders ached and his chest felt tight and a bit sore. The damp hut wasn't helping, but he had noticed the tightness in his chest once or twice recently and it seemed to have worsened after the long Brunswick op the day before. It was hot and stuffy in his wireless operator's post as the heating duct outlet was right next to where he sat – but then every time he had to move around the aircraft to do jobs, he had to enter the freezing cold sections too. Plus it was impossible to cart the oxygen cylinder around with him – the blasted thing never seemed to work – so he found himself wheezing and gasping for breath more often than not.

He coughed again and flung off the coarse blanket, dragging himself out of the narrow bed. Though it was sunny it was still very chilly, and the thought of shaving in cold water made him shiver. He knew that whiskers and oxygen masks didn't mix, so he steeled himself and splashed his face, chasing away all remnants of sleep. Picking up his brush, he tried to tame his wavy brown hair. He'd been given the brush back in 1942 at Padgate when he was being kitted out yet he could recall that day as clearly as if it was yesterday. He could even taste the proud thrill he had felt when he was given his prized possession, the "white flash" that he wore in his cap to show he was air crew under training. Duncan glanced at the brush. He'd written his service number on it, right underneath the manufacturer's details: "C. Leng and Sons Ltd. 1941. Warranted All Bristles". He remembered with a wry smile how some of his army friends back home had called him a "Brylcreem Boy" – the slang name they gave to the RAF crew on account of their smartness and slicked back hair. Ginger's voice interrupted his reminiscences.

"Are you coming to the mess for breakfast, Dunc?"

"On my way" he replied.

Breakfast was porridge. Porridge and gossip. There was a buzz that another op was on the cards and judging by what the driver of one of the fuel dowsers had said (or so the story went) it would be a very long flight, as all the aircraft were to carry the maximum load of aviation fuel. The gossip was soon proved correct. After a short pre-briefing, Duncan and Ginger joined the rest of their crew at the dispersal for pre-flight checks on H-How. Their final destination hadn't yet been announced, but they all knew it was somewhere deep inside enemy territory. When the crews were back at their respective messes, a loud Tannoy broadcast announced the time of the full briefing.

The room was packed, as each man held his breath waiting to hear the target. It was Munich. The news brought with it the realisation that it really would be an arduous undertaking due to the lengthy flying time involved – around ten hours. So, for the fourth time in just a few days, the airmen collected their parachutes, helmets and flying gear. They handed over their valuables in exchange for their escape kits and they each collected their rations of sandwiches, chunks of chocolate, barley sugar sweets and flasks of hot tea or coffee. It would have to last them a long time.

Although the day had begun bright, it had become dull during the afternoon and by the early evening thicker clouds had built up. A few spots of rain spattered the windscreen of the truck that was driving Chas and his crew to the dispersal point. Duncan coughed and, with a shiver, pulled up his collar to ward off the evening chill. The truck pulled up alongside H-How and the crew climbed out, ready for their final checks. Although there was a familiarity of routine about it all, their fears and uncertainties were fresh and tangible. There is such a fine line between being the lucky ones who will survive and being those on whom fortune does not smile. Would they be climbing back into their beds that night, or would someone come in and roll up their mattresses, as they had all seen done too many times in the past few weeks?

It was better to occupy one's mind and push out dark thoughts. Chas and Paddy Duggan, the flight engineer walked round H-How, checking the wings and studs, then the engine covers and finally the rudders. They all climbed inside the narrow fuselage and made their way through its claustrophobic interior, the central spar causing fresh bruises on several shins as each man, except for Ginger, clambered across to his position. Then it was ignition on, as the fitter in charge of the accumulator battery outside the aircraft, just below the wing, shouted "Contact" and Paddy Duggan pressed one of the black starter buttons. The first engine sputtered, choked, whirred and then roared into life. H-How joined the rest of the Lancasters and within twenty minutes they were on their way. As the last aircraft lifted off the runway at Skellingthorpe and was enveloped in the cloudy canyons above, the little groups of well-wishers on the ground thrust their hands into their pockets and shuffled back into the community buildings. In the control tower, the flight times were chalked up on the wall display. Skellingthorpe was quiet. The Lancasters had gone. The airmen – the life and soul of the place – were all up in the skies. Silence ruled. Prayers were understood but unspoken.

First they flew east, then south and back over land again, crossing Essex to join the rest of the bomber stream midway over the English Channel. Two hundred and forty four Lancasters droned through the dark skies, ever mindful of the possibility of collision. Across the sea, over the flak batteries, and onward, ever nearer. Over France and then southern Germany the land was deepest black: no lights shone to give a bearing or a semblance of location. In the near distance to their right, like a sea of starlight dropped from the sky, lay Switzerland. Neutral and inviolate, her lights shimmered like a Christmas tree, a poignant reminder of happier times.

H-How flew on, as they neared their target they could see a barrage of flak in the distance ahead, vivid bursts among a forest of swirling searchlight beams. There was no turning back, no way out, they simply had to carry on and fly right into it, straight into the mouth of the tiger. There was no time to give in to the terror of it, for it was upon them. The maze of searchlights grew brighter and bigger – sometimes they appeared to be in small groups, but the most fearful were the cones. These were made up of twenty or more beams that would focus together, their apex filled with scarlet bursts of heavy flak. The cones often held a victim ensnared, almost hypnotised, as if pinned to the sky.

Duncan had climbed into the astrodome and could see one poor devil coned. The aircraft appeared to be twisting and corkscrewing to try and shake off the searchlights and the surrounding flak that was bursting all around. Then, as Duncan watched horrified, he saw a red flicker shoot out from one of the stricken aircraft's wings, followed by a huge ball of flame. Suddenly he saw a parachute, it appeared to hit the tail of the aircraft and then spun off to one side. It drifted away, a lifeless shape below it, gently spiralling thousands of feet to the earth below. Duncan watched, horrified, silently begging the other crewmen to bale out, but there were no more. The flak was everywhere around them now. Flashes of red, orange, and yellow. Angry flashes of brilliant light that seemed to leap everywhere without warning. He could see it, he could smell it, he could hear it, he could taste it. Cruel searchlight beams scythed at the air around H-How. Duncan quickly returned to his wireless operator's post.

The first indication of imminent danger was seven, maybe more, heavy shells ringing their aircraft. Then came a second salvo, fast and loud. What to do? A turn to the left or to the right, a climb, or a dive could just as easily carry them into the next burst. The decision was made by circumstance. The usual darkness inside H-How was suddenly transformed into blue-white brilliance as twenty beams of intense luminosity focused on them. They were ablaze with light so bright that it was momentarily blinding. They were coned. Trapped. Helpless victims awaiting slaughter. Exploding flak burst all around them. It was terrifying. In just a second the guns would zero in on H-How and rip it to shreds.

Then they were hit. On the starboard wing, the outer engine was torn apart. Splinters of exploded steel were everywhere, crashing into the wings and the fuselage. Whether it was a night fighter or the flak batteries that hit them – who knows?

Chas's reaction was instant. He plunged the Lancaster into a violent corkscrew dive, descending so fast that his nose bled. The aircraft went downwards hard, then right over till its wings were almost vertical. A roll the other way, then round again and down further. The gunners were pinned inside their constricted turrets. In the bomb aimer's bubble, Ben Lawrence held on for dear life as he watched the ground nauseatingly spiral upwards toward him.

"Bloody hell, the starboard outer engine's on fire, Skipper," yelled Paddy, as crimson tongues licked around the wing.

"Kill it, fast" shouted Chas, as Paddy, not waiting to be told, throttled the engine back and feathered its propellers. He knew full well that they had less than three minutes before the flames would spread and the fuel tanks would ignite. His gloved fingers located the red fire extinguisher button; he pushed it, praying, and the flames died.

The Lancaster's remaining three engines screamed in agony, as the stricken aircraft plunged in a ten thousand foot descent through the air, away from the combined death-grip of the searchlights and the flak. Chas wrenched at the controls, wrestling H-How out of the danger zone. When they had dropped to an altitude of eight thousand feet, gasping with exhaustion, he began to level the Lancaster out. The sheer physical effort that he had put into corkscrewing the heavy aircraft through the skies had been immense. He found that he was drenched with sweat and the muscles in his shoulders and forearms were hot with pain. But there was no time to even think about that.

Suddenly, as the aircraft levelled, the negative gravity force kicked in. Duncan gripped his chair tightly to stop himself from being flung across the fuselage. The air was full of flying pencils, flasks, maps and odd bits of paper. In the way that small incidentals can occupy one's mind when utter terror and fear are so enormous that they are almost blotted out, Duncan reached to grab his thermos flask as it floated past him. Death may be imminent, but he was damned if he was going to lose his hot drink.

Then darkness. The violent corkscrewing descent had put such a strain on the engines that they had blown the generator out. All electrical power to the aircraft had been lost. No lights, no hydraulics, no navigation – nothing. Duncan forgot about his flask and thought fast. He knew they'd been taught about something like this during training, if only he could recall what on earth it was. His mind raced.

"Got it," he muttered excitedly, " it has to be a master fuse".

On the starboard side of the cabin wall was a bank of master fuses; fumbling he opened it up and shone his torch inside, hoping to find replacements. He silently vowed to buy the rigger a pint of beer when (if) they next met up, as fortunately the chap had kitted H-How out properly with the replacement fuses. Duncan thanked his lucky stars and got to work. The distant whine of the generator starting up could just be heard over the engines, as the cabin lights flickered back on. Chas briefly called his thanks over the intercom. But there was no time now to dwell on what had just transpired – they were almost over the target, flying at low altitude on three engines and with a full bomb load. Ben began calling out his instructions.

"Skip, we're almost there. Target markers ahead, we're so low I can see them very clearly. Left, Skipper, left, left. Right a bit."

The Lancaster released its massive load, soaring upwards as the bombs dropped. Flying at just eight thousand feet, their present danger wasn't so much from the flak batteries below, but was instead from other bombs being dropped by the RAF Lancasters flying above them. It wouldn't have been the first time that an inadvertent friendly bomb load had put paid to an unlucky aircraft. Chas banked as quickly as he could on three engines, for the loss of power on the starboard side made maneouvering the heavy plane very difficult. Now their main problem was getting back home – a six hour flight against a head wind, on only three engines.

They stayed low and kept their airspeed down, it wasn't possible to gain altitude even if they'd wanted to. Chas was cool and very determined. He'd got them out of one almost certain catastrophe, he was damned if he was going to quit now. They were going to get back to Skellingthorpe. They really were on a wing and a prayer – and he'd give it as many prayers as it took.

Six hours seemed like sixty. Night turned into day. Eventually they limped back. Never had the runway at Skellingthorpe seemed so welcoming. Never had the faces of the riggers, who met them after they had been marshalled to their dispersal point, seemed so friendly. Never had the crackle from the Lancaster's three white hot exhausts seemed so re-assuring. Never had their coffee and cigarettes tasted so sweet.

Their elation was heady and intoxicating, like a drug. They were home.

CHAPTER TWENTY SIX

The damage to H-How was severe. It's odd how human beings can relate to an inanimate object, but they undoubtedly do. Chas and his crew had become used to H-How, and they trusted her. She'd carried them through some of the most dangerous skies imaginable – and she had returned them safely. She was a lucky talisman of sorts, having limped back to base despite undergoing fearful attacks. When they learned the next day that she would have to be taken out of service because she was so badly damaged, they were not happy.

But there was no time for sentiment of any sort. They were given a new aircraft and sent out immediately on several short training flights to familiarise themselves. Within twenty four hours 50 Squadron had to be ready to depart on another long mission. It was not an auspicious destination, for it was to be Schweinfurt, close to Nuremburg, the scene of one of the RAF's recent dreadful losses.

In fact the overall plan for the night was to carry out not one, but three raids. The major one was to Essen, the second one was to a railway target at Villeneuve-St-Georges and the third (using 50 Squadron) was to Schweinfurt. It was assumed that the large Essen force would attract the attention of the German night-fighters, but it didn't work out quite that way. The smaller group heading for Schweinfurt met unexpectedly strong head winds that delayed them and further exposed them to the brunt of the *Luftwaffe's* fierce attacks.

Over twenty allied aircraft from that smaller group that flew to Schweinfurt were wiped out that night. On one of that twenty, a spectacular act of bravery took place. It was the sort of thing that can make the hairs on the back of your neck tingle and stand up if you have the kind of imagination that allows you to visualise even a tiny part of the events. It was the sort of thing that can make your jaw go slack with amazement when you read it. It was the sort of thing that happens in films, but surely never really happens in everyday life. But this was no everyday life, no ordinary time. Yet the actions were performed by everyday people – young men – many of them barely in their twenties.

So what actually was that act of bravery? The details are known today because several of the crew survived to tell the tale. There were many other acts of heroism and sacrifice – not only on that night, but also on so very many other, similar nights – but so often those stories of heroism would never be told. Consigned to oblivion. Incinerated, immolated, lost in a thousand conflagrations. Scorched onto tongues that would never speak again. Known only by souls that have slipped away into oblivion.

Let this tale serve for all those tales that will never be known. Let this be the testimonial of courage for all the eyes that no longer see, and all the mouths that forever remain silent.

Flak or fighter cannon fire caused a blaze close to one of the petrol tanks on the starboard wing of one of the bombers. Realising they were all doomed unless action was taken quickly, their flight engineer, twenty five year old Sergeant Norman Jackson, volunteered to climb out onto the vast wing of the Lancaster with a fire extinguisher, and try to put out the flames.

Think about it. They were 20,000 feet up and moving through the night at over 200 mph. Once he had climbed out, there was no simple way back inside the aircraft for Jackson, and he knew it. He chose to risk his own life in a terrifying manner, for his fellow crewmen. He strapped on his parachute and crawled out through the pilot's escape hatch into the intense freezing cold air. Moving out along the wing with the fire extinguisher stuffed inside his tunic, he drew ever nearer to the fierce flames. A *Luftwaffe* fighter appeared and strafed the Lancaster with cannon fire, wounding Jackson and causing the heavy bomber to manouever wildly. It was an impossible mission. Jackson was swept through the flames, his hands and face badly burned – he plummeted from the burning wing with his parachute partly open and on fire. Miraculously he survived, though badly injured and was later awarded the Victoria Cross for his bravery.

This tale was told. Many other events of bravery and sacrifice will never be known.

For Chas, Ben, Duncan, Ginger and the others in their new Lancaster, the night was another one of hell. Their recent experience of being coned and shot made them feel more vulnerable, more exposed. Until you're hit you think "it'll never happen to me". And then it does, and you know that it can so easily, oh so very easily, be you. In fact, having escaped from what seemed to be your terrible fate, you even wonder if by cheating death previously, you may have encouraged it to seek you out the next time. As Chas corkscrewed their aircraft away from the snare of the searchlights, every man prayed to his God and thought long and hard of his wife, or his sweetheart, his family, his friends and his past. Each man was aware how fine the line was that might place him to one side or the other of certain death. And so they prayed – and that night they survived.

By the end of the month they were exhausted, but there was no let up, for this was a crucial time during the run-up to what would later be known as D-Day. There were ops to St-Médard-en-Jalles, Toulouse and then, on the night of May 3rd., to Mailly-le-Camp (where the French Resistance had discovered a Panzer tank concentration at a military base). But oh what a terrible mess that mission turned out to be. The aim was sound, but the execution was sadly lacking. And ironically, execution, of a sort, became the fate of over forty Lancasters that night.

The RAF official records state that "control of this raid in the target area failed to operate according to plan". What happened was that the crews spent over two hours flying round and round the target area awaiting instructions because the main controller's radio communications were not operating correctly. The Lancasters circled, waiting and waiting – desperate to get the job done and quit the area as soon as possible. Almost four hundred massive aircraft were forced to orbit the area together, trying to avoid each other in the dark skies. Meanwhile, the *Luftwaffe* fighters had plenty of time to come in and seek out their prey. And of course, that's exactly what they did.

It had been a beautiful spring night in northern France; lit by a thousand stars and with a moon shining high bathing the countryside in a milky softness. The inhabitants of the area around Mailly-le-Camp had witnessed the terrible scenes above them, as the heavy bombers roared overhead, pursued by agile fighter aircraft. One man watched in horror as a Lancaster in flames, like an airborne torch, screamed downwards. A massive explosion rent the air as the aircraft crashed to earth in woodland, with its full bomb load still intact. For miles around in the little villages, windows shattered and roof tiles tumbled off. An opaque red cloud rose up from the ground where the plane had impacted – the trees crackled and burned.

The nights continued. One merged into the next. There were attacks on ammunition dumps, port installations, submarines and communication links. The weeks were being counted down to D-day, though only a privileged few were aware of the forthcoming planned events. There was a brief scare when a Lancaster, carrying a rather special senior officer as second pilot, was shot down. The officer in question was a base commander who had only just taken up his position, his previous post being a high-up staff job in which he had had access to details of the coming invasion. There were fears and much anxiety amongst the "powers-that-be" in case he released any secrets, should he have survived and been captured. With hindsight, we have the privilege of knowing that no secrets were divulged. Indeed he was taken prisoner, but his importance was not discovered. The D-Day invasion plans remained safe.

There was no let up. The attacks and the bombardment were relentless. Exhausted crews were sent home briefly so that they might re-energise themselves, ready for the next onslaught. In mid May, Chas and his crew were granted leave after nineteen gruelling operations. Duncan wearily packed his kit bag and set out to walk into Lincoln to get the train. He knew he didn't have the energy to ride his bike to the station. His shoulders were aching and he was racked with coughing spasms, but he had to see Pauline. Nothing else mattered.

CHAPTER TWENTY SEVEN

The packed train rumbled along, crossing several sets of points near Crewe with a series of jolts. The sudden movement disturbed Duncan from a fitful sleep. He woke, coughing and struggling for breath; the pain in his shoulder blades made him gasp. A thick-set man in a trilby opposite shot him a look of sympathy, while the white haired matron who was in the seat next to him, did her best to increase the distance between herself and the pale looking airman.

The carriage was packed. The railway was the only way that people could travel over long distances, as petrol for cars was rationed. It was available to few sectors of the general public, for example those who performed essential duties such as doctors. Any other private car owners (and there were precious few) simply couldn't get hold of the petrol, effectively putting their vehicles out of action for some considerable time.

When the thundering train finally pulled into Manchester's Central Station, with a succession of loud hisses and roars, Duncan was exhausted. He waited till most of the rest of the people in the carriage had moved into the corridor and were piling out of the train, anxious to get to their final destinations. Heaving his kit bag down from the rack above his head was an effort and the man in the trilby (who had hung back from the rest of the carriage's previous occupants) stretched out his arm to help wrestle it down.

"Steady on airman" he gently warned Duncan. "You don't look too fit. Are you OK?"

"I'll be fine" replied Duncan, grateful for the kindness. The man patted him on the back and left the carriage. Duncan hoisted his old kit bag onto his shoulder, wincing at the pain that the movement caused, and followed him off the train.

When Pauline saw Duncan she knew right away that he was ill. He'd lost weight and looked gaunt, but it was his face that troubled her most. His usually ruddy and healthy complexion was pale and drawn. She put up her fingers to touch his cheek and was shocked at his hot, dry skin. She placed her palm on his forehead and knew that he was burning with fever. Her pleading that he should visit the doctor immediately fell on deaf ears. The last thing Duncan wanted to do was waste precious time on leave by sitting in the doctor's surgery. He assured her (with a conviction that he didn't truly feel) that he would be fine.

But that night he grew worse. Sleep was impossible. His shoulders were sore, he had a cold sweat and was obviously running a fever. Rasping and grating coughing spasms racked his body. Then the chest pains began. Severe and crippling, their fierceness was at its height when he coughed. Pauline did her best to help, and finally at around five in the morning, he fell into a fitful sleep.

There was no escaping a visit to the doctor this time. Duncan dragged his weary body to the doctor's surgery and sat on the hard wooden bench. The waiting room was full, mainly with mothers and children, some of whom looked very frail. Times were hard and rationing had been in place for years now – there were little children in the room who had spent the entirety of their short lives on rationed food. Even soap was rationed, and no one was allowed to bathe in water more than five inches deep, though it didn't look as if that bothered some of the little urchins Duncan could see in the room. He smiled, remembering himself at that age, and his thoughts went back to his mother. He wondered if she would have been proud of him in his RAF blue uniform. Duncan inhaled deeply with a sigh and instantly doubled up with pain.

It seemed an eternity before the doctor finally saw him, and then it was hard to concentrate on what was being said. Following a brief physical examination, the doctor advised Duncan to return back to his base while he still had the strength to do so. To be signed off as unfit for duty (which the doctor realised was essential) it was necessary that Duncan had to be seen by RAF medical staff at Skellingthorpe. It was surely pneumonia and pleurisy, but it was imperative that he should get back to Lincolnshire.

Feverish, wracked with pain and exhaustion, Duncan once again boarded the steam train for yet another long journey. Pauline was distraught at seeing him go; he was so weak and obviously very sick indeed. He tried to reassure her, but it wasn't easy, for whenever he tried to talk he was constantly interrupted by paroxysms of coughing that further served to underline his predicament. She knew that, once he had left, it would be days if not weeks before she next heard from him. She prayed that she *would* hear from him. Prayed that the next missive would be in his familiar hand and not typed, or worse, that it might, please God, not be a telegram. The dreaded telegram informing the family that their beloved was no more.

Their parting was agony, the journey was long and painful. As he got off the train at Lincoln, Duncan was close to the point of collapse. By a stroke of luck he got a lift back to Skellingthorpe. He reported to the duty officer, and asked to see the doctor, but words really weren't necessary. One look at the ashen faced young airman, beads of sweat covering his skin, his body wracked with pain, sufficed. The diagnosis was swiftly made: a serious pleural effusion and pneumonia. He was sent to the Military Hospital in Lincoln, where X ray examination indicated his heart had been displaced to the side by the mass of fluid in his chest cavity. Officially declared unfit for duty, Duncan was immediately consigned to a hospital bed.

The following twenty four hours became a blur. The fever and pain blanked out mostly everything else. Then, the day after, Chas came to visit Duncan in the hospital and was instantly shocked by his cadaverous appearance. The illness had certainly taken its toll. His face was drawn and yellowish in colour, the bones starkly chiselled above sunken cheeks. His eyes, usually twinkling and eager, were dull and watery. When he saw Chas, his face lit up for a moment, and he struggled to sit up, stretching out his hand to take the pilot's proffered warm clasp.

"Dunc, you look washed out. How are you doing?" Chas gently enquired, though one look at his sick crewman had already provided the answer to the question.

"I'm fine, I want to come back with you Chas. I want to fly. I want to be with you and Ben and Ginger. But they've said I'm unfit for duty". Duncan gasped with the exertion of sitting up and speaking.

"I've talked to your doctors, Dunc. There's not a chance of you flying for a while, you know. You're really ill and they need to keep you in hospital for a few more weeks yet."

Chas understood Duncan's desperate eagerness to join his fellow crew, but it was an impossible desire. He was undoubtedly a very sick man. In his heart Chas had a feeling that Duncan wouldn't be flying with him again, but he couldn't bring himself to say that to his dear friend.

Duncan fell back against the hard pillows, exhausted, his face pale with pain and strained with emotion. He knew Chas was right. He knew he couldn't leave the hospital, but there was something driving him, making him want to plead, he felt he just had to fly with Chas and the lads the next time. But it was futile, pointless. His mind knew the facts but his heart wasn't listening.

Chas chatted to Duncan for a short while, trying to raise his spirits and take both their minds off the situation. The ward was stuffy and the air oppressive with the characteristic smell of disinfectant. He joked to Duncan that at least the smell was better than the unpleasant rubber of the oxygen masks they all wore on the Lancaster. They both smiled. Neither airman noticed the ward sister approach them, despite the rustling of her starched apron. "I'm sorry Sir" she said, patting a loose tendril of hair into her white headdress as she addressed Chas, a pretty pink blush tinting her usually pallid complexion. "I'm afraid you'll have to go now – the Sergeant is very ill and needs to get some rest".

Chas gave her a half smile – she was only doing her job – but it was a wrench to leave Duncan there. He gritted his teeth – now was not the time to be weak. He clasped Duncan's hand in his own strong grasp. "I'll see you soon" he promised, yet his dark eyes held a haunted look.

The pilot's departing steps echoed around the hospital ward. As Duncan watched his friend go, the emotional ache in his heart was almost as bad as the pains in his chest and lungs from the pleurisy. He closed his eyes. He would write a letter to Chas thanking him for coming to the hospital to visit. One of the nurses would surely post it for him tomorrow – it would be waiting for Chas when he returned to Skellingthorpe after the next op.

Chapter Twenty Eight

When Chas woke the next day, his first thought was of Duncan. It was such a lovely day; he felt sorry for him trapped inside the stuffy hospital ward, where you simply couldn't take a deep breath without choking on the thick stench of disinfectant.

And it really was a lovely day. A beautiful May day. The sun was warm on the emerald green grass, sending little shivers of early morning mist upwards; tendrils of dawn chasing away the wraiths of the night. White May blossom, sometimes tinted with shades of deep rose-pink, glistened against the dark green of the hedgerows, to become (as H. E. Bates eloquently wrote) "the risen cream of all the milkiness of May-time".

May blossom, always so pretty in the wild, yet considered unlucky to be brought inside the home. Woodland hawthorn blossom has a distinctive heady perfume, but folklore says that it gives off an unpleasant scent of death soon after it is cut. Not all the blossoms were to be seen in the shrubby hedgerows. Here and there were small, gnarled trees bearing hawthorn flowers that were blood red, like carmine – intense and deep. In the shady undergrowth was the ivy, its new fresh leaves mingling with the brown, decaying mulch of the previous autumn. Dappled shadows played kiss chase with each other, rippling from tree to tree, while majestic horse chestnuts with their candle-like blossoms held aloft, laden and full, stood guardian over the beauty of it all.

It really was a lovely day.

But war pays no heed to lovely days. At Skellingthorpe, 50 Squadron were given their instructions for an op that night, to Brunswick. Chas was assigned a "spare bod" called George, a young Scots lad, in Duncan's place as wireless operator. At the full briefing, he was introduced to the rest of the crew. Hands were shaken, brief smiles exchanged and the usual black jokes made. But they all missed Duncan.

Duncan belonged. He was one of their team. Duncan was part of their family.

The lovely day grew cooler and the shadows lengthened. Evening came and the bomber crews were driven out to the waiting aircraft at the dispersals. Chas climbed on board his Lancaster, followed by Paddy Duggan and Ben. They all ducked as they clambered inside the fuselage, so as to avoid the low metal beams. Nav Linton followed a moment or two later, with Ernie McIlwaine hot on his heels and the new man, George, clambering up behind.

"Damn it" cursed George, forgetting to duck as he entered the aircraft, and smacking his head on the metal beam. He put his hand to his forehead and wiped away a small trickle of blood. "Damn".

"Bad luck, old man," joked Ginger, as he followed George up the ladder, trying to make light of the situation. Chas looked back and a momentary shadow darkened his face.

The calm of the quiet May evening was soon destroyed by the thunderous roar of the massed Merlin engines, as one by one the Lancasters took off, soaring over the flat Lincolnshire countryside and out towards the North Sea. In his hospital bed, Duncan could only listen. Hearing the distinctive roar as they passed overhead only increased his feeling of isolation. He felt as incomplete as he did when he wasn't with Pauline. But at that moment he ached to be in the plane with his friends, with Chas, Ben and the others. It was where he belonged. He shut his eyes and prayed.

When the bomber crews reached Brunswick they found that the weather forecast they'd been given for the area was wrong.

The predicted clear target was completely covered by cloud; the raid was also dogged by problems caused by interference on the Master Bomber's radio communications. Things seemed to go wrong, the target markers fell in the wrong place and the entire raid was unsuccessful. The aircraft all turned for home, praying that the coastal flak defences and the ever watchful *Luftwaffe* wouldn't wreak their revenge.

As they neared the coast of Holland, Ginger thought he caught a glimpse of a grey shape below them. It was so sudden. He looked again. Nothing. Below them, about a hundred feet away, the unseen *Messerchmitt* 110 pilot took his time to line up the cross hairs of his gun sight neatly with the space between the two engines on the bomber's starboard wing. He pushed the trigger button and six streams of cannon fire blasted forth, hitting the Lancaster's fuel tanks. The *Messerchmitt* dropped back, diving, not wanting to be caught up in the blazing annihilation that would surely follow in moments. *Schrage Musik* – the perfect execution.

In his tail end turret, Ginger saw a river of fire streaming past his left side, out into the black night. With trembling hands he forced open the turret doors behind him and stared into the roaring hell of crimson flame that had become the fuselage of their aircraft.

"Chas! Ben ….. " he screamed into the cauldron of fire.

A massive explosion ripped the Lancaster apart. Then there was nothing.

CHAPTER TWENTY NINE

POST OFFICE TELEGRAM STOP
I DEEPLY REGRET TO INFORM YOU THAT YOUR
SON IS MISSING AND BELIEVED DEAD STOP

Dear Pauline

I'm so sorry about Duncan. You must be heartbroken. They were all such wonderful boys. I had the terrible telegram last week telling me that Eric was missing. I couldn't believe it, I have hardly stopped crying since. I just wanted to let you know how sorry I am for you, about Duncan.

Yours truly, Emily

Dear Chas

I'm just writing to let you know that I've been transferred from Lincoln Military Hospital to Rauceby RAF Hospital. It's about twenty miles away, so I know you won't be able to visit me there.

I want to thank you again for coming to see me last week. I wrote to you the day after you came, but I know you won't have had any time to reply to me yet.

Tell the rest of the gang that I miss you all. I'm trying to get them to discharge me but even though I'm feeling a bit better, they say it will be a few months yet before I can get out.

Dunc

Dearest Pauline

I've written two letters to Chas, but he hasn't replied. Then today, the first letter that I wrote about ten days ago (the day he came to visit me in Lincoln Hospital) was sent back to me. I don't understand it. Why would it have come back to me?

I'm worried Pauline. I'm worried that something has happened to them all. Nobody here seems to know and I don't know how to find out. They won't let me leave so there's nothing I can do.

I'm feeling a little bit better now and they say the fever has gone, but they won't let me get up out of bed yet. They've given me a lumbar puncture and took two pints of fluid off my lungs. They said my heart had been displaced by two inches.

I wish that I could see you. Everything would be all right then, I know.

All my love
Dunc

My darling Duncan

I don't know how to tell you this. I wish that I could hold you tight as I explain it to you, but I can't, so these words will have to suffice.

Chas and the rest of the crew did not return to Skellingthorpe after their op on May 22nd. That was the day after Chas came to visit you in hospital at Lincoln. They are missing presumed dead. Ginger's mother wrote to me. It was awful. She didn't know that you were sick and in hospital, so she thought that you had been on the op too. She thought you were dead as well. Her letter was so sad, it made me cry. Oh Duncan, I don't know what to say to her, but I will have to write back. It's just so awful. I'm beside myself with grief.

All my love forever
Pauline

Dear Emily

This is very hard for me to write, but I have to do so. Duncan is in hospital and has been there since May 20th. He came home on leave the week before and was very ill. On his return to Skellingthorpe the doctors sent him straight to hospital with serious chest problems (pleural effusion and pneumonia). He is still in hospital and I expect him to be there for some months yet. He was not with Chas and the crew on the night of May 22nd.

I am so deeply sorry, Emily, about the loss of your dear son. He was such a wonderful person. Duncan thought the world of him.

We are saying prayers for you, dear Emily.

Sincerely

Pauline.

I can't believe it. My darling son George only went on one op with this crew as a replacement wireless operator. It was his first time with them. Now he's missing, you say he's dead. He shouldn't have been there. It was the first time he had gone with them. Why did it happen? It shouldn't have been him. It's not right. It's just not right.

Official records.
50 Squadron
LL744 (May 22, 1944)

Missing in action, presumed dead:

Flight Lieutenant George Charles Startin, Royal Australian Air Force

Flight Sergeant Keith Gilbert Lawrence, Royal Air Force

Sergeant Eric Hopkinson, Royal Air Force Volunteer Reserve

Sergeant Daniel Patrick Duggan, Royal Air Force Volunteer Reserve

Sergeant George Reid, Royal Air Force Volunteer Reserve

Bodies recovered from North Sea coast.

Sergeant (Air Gnr.) William Ernest McIlwaine, Royal Air Force Volunteer Reserve. (Buried Bergen Op Zoom War Cemetery, Netherlands)

Pilot Officer (Nav.) Francis Malcolm Linton, Royal Canadian Air Force. (Buried Sage War Cemetery, Germany)

Rest in Peace

EPILOGUE

It was a Tuesday in early November, and one of those bright days when the sky is a delicious pale blue and the leaves underfoot crunch crisply when you walk on them. It was the sort of day when it feels really great to be alive. As I walked toward the supermarket entrance I could see the man. He was young, maybe nineteen or perhaps twenty. He looked smart, dressed in his RAF blue uniform, in stark contrast to the casual attire of most of the shoppers in their jeans and trainers. I fumbled around in my bag for my purse, as it was a personal rule of mine to always buy a poppy on Remembrance Day. The least I could do.

The young man was busy, for most passers-by were pushing coins into his collecting box. Our little Hampshire market town was renowned for being generous to good causes – shown by the plethora of charity shops like "Scope" and "Help the Aged" that overflowed with donated paperbacks, twee ornaments and yesterday's fashion mistakes. I took two pound coins from my purse, shoving the loose till receipts back into its overflowing innards, reminding myself in the process that I had a coupon I must use when I filled the car up with petrol. My mind was doing its usual multi-tasking between thinking what I needed to buy for supper, not forgetting to pick up the DVD I'd ordered and making sure I used that money off coupon when I called in at the petrol station on the way home. I handed over the coins to the young RAF man and smiled at him as he handed me a blood red poppy in return.

And it was then that I stopped in my tracks. On the table in front of the young man was a pile of RAF postcards and stickers, stacked alongside a variety of advertising literature and other assorted paraphernalia, all fronted by a small draped banner bearing the familiar message "Lest We Forget".

I gazed at the postcards.

"Can I have one of those please – er, how much does it cost?" I pointed at the card I wanted.

"Oh yes, take it please, you can have one free". He smiled, and handed me the card.

"It's a Lancaster you see" I explained to him; though he must have wondered why I felt the need to clarify my reasoning. "My father flew in a Lancaster in the war" I unaccountably continued to justify myself.

The man smiled again and nodded, but I was lost in my own thoughts and I didn't pay him the attention that his gentle politeness should have earned. I stared at the postcard and the dark form that was starkly printed on the white background.

Avro Lancaster B Mk 1, proclaimed the printed title. I read the explanatory detail on the reverse of the card. *The name Lancaster is synonymous with many famous actions during World War II but it is perhaps best remembered as the bomber aircraft which turned the tide and remains to this day, in the Battle of Britain Memorial Flight, linked with the Hurricane and Spitfire which performed with equal distinction in the fighter role earlier in the war.*

I slipped the postcard carefully inside my bag with the poppy and collected a metal trolley from the serried ranks lined up like tin soldiers outside the crowded shop entrance. Then I shopped. I got most of the stuff I needed, forgot to get the DVD, forgot to fill up the car with petrol, drove home, unloaded the shopping, emptied the bags, filled the fridge, made a coffee, then sat down and looked at the postcard.

The Avro Lancaster. My eyes travelled over its distinctive shape, with the gun turrets, astrodome and bomb aimers' compartments. How many secrets, how many untold memories, fears and hopes had their final resting place inside its metal walls? I stroked the outline of the shape on the postcard. Then I went to fetch my Christening cup and my old watch. They'd both been tucked away inside a drawer for many years. Precious items for sure, but until that day neither fully appreciated nor understood by me (their recipient and custodian).

The Christening cup had travelled half way round the world when it was first posted, to mark my baptism. Made of electro plated nickel silver, and marked underneath *Lewbury*, it was engraved with my name and the words:

From Mr and Mrs Startin, Australia, Christmas 1949

Chas's Mum and Dad. I held the little cup in my hands, marvelling at the warmth and generosity of spirit that had been felt all those years ago by two lonely people who had lost their beloved only son, half a world away.

Then I picked up the watch. It no longer had a strap, so couldn't be worn, and it didn't work, but it had had plenty of use throughout the years. When I was eleven and attending high school, my father had given it to me with a simple request to take care of it. It was precious. I wore it through my years at school, only swapping it later when it seemed a little too cumbersome for my budding fashion awareness. It was a good watch, Swiss made, a badge of repute.

My father had told me that it had been his mother's watch. Agnes. She had been given it for her twenty first birthday and when she died it had been the one thing that my father had that was hers. He wore it every day. He wore it on every op, on every mission that he undertook in the Lancaster. He was wearing it the day that he first met Chas, Ben, Ginger and the rest – when hands were shaken and friendships begun. Friendships that would never die.

For many years, first as a young child growing up in the post war Baby Boom years – and then as a teenager and student, full of principles and ideals, I had not wanted to know about the war that had almost taken away my father. I thought only of the future, not realising how deeply it is intertwined with the past. Life sped by, I had children, and as they grew I learned the truth of valuing another's life greater than my own.

But until that day when I looked with fresh eyes at the picture of the aircraft that had been both my father's salvation and the sepulchre of his friends, I simply hadn't fully understood.

~ ~ ~

My father had been utterly distraught when he had received confirmation of the fate of his fellow crew members, in late May, 1944. He'd been pre-occupied by a desperate feeling of unease when his first letter to Chas was returned unopened. No amount of supposedly logical argument that the postman had simply mixed things up could convince him. In his heart, he knew that the worst had happened, and his weakened, sick body couldn't bear the grief. When he received the letter from my mother telling him what he dreaded most was true, he wept until he could weep no more. Guilt at not dying with them was uppermost in his mind. There was no relief at having been spared by a quirk of fate. He had simply wished he were dead.

Then came other nightmares to test his sanity. Spectres from hell. "If only you had been there on that op to Brunswick" whispered the bogeymen "you could have saved them". Maybe it wouldn't have happened, maybe things would have been different. Cross your fingers, bid good day to the magpie, throw spilled salt over your left shoulder (it must be your left) – all superstitions that have no logic. Sleep brought an end to the torments of his waking thoughts, and replaced them with the agonies that come in dreams. Cruel dreams, the nature of which, no one should have to endure.

From the Military Hospital in Lincoln, he had been transferred to Rauceby RAF Hospital. He felt as if his life was at an end. By day his mind would go over the events of the past few weeks, with a series of "if onlys" and "I might haves". As night approached he would dread the onset of the dark, knowing what form his thoughts would take.

The nursing staff were wonderful, they'd seen many like Duncan, men whose comrades had died. Their efficiency and practical attitude helped him to get through the first few days. Dressed in hospital blue, with a regular air force shirt under a bright blue cotton jacket or dressing gown, each patient also wore his stripes on an elastic armband. When the weather was pleasant, they would be taken outside in wheelchairs onto a balcony where many would simply stare at the sky.

Another young sergeant in the hospital also had pleurisy and pneumonia, the same as my father. He never talked but seemed to be wrapped up in himself and his problems, though he would never share them. At meal times my father watched him and noticed that he hardly ate, but just picked at the food on his plate, shifting it around with listless abandon. As the days passed my father realised that the young man had simply given up on himself, or worse, had given up on life. He was losing weight rapidly, practically shrivelling away in front of everyone's eyes. He no longer wanted to live.

It was a terrible waste; another life sacrificed – and for what? Observing him, and realising that this was not how it should be, my father came to a decision that would save his own sanity. He made a vow. A vow to Chas, Ben and Ginger, to Nav, Ernie and Paddy and to the young "spare bod" called George who had taken Duncan's fateful place on the doomed Brunswick flight. A vow to the families of each of those men, to keep their memory alive. Never, ever to forget. No matter what.

And so the months passed. Rauceby was too far for Pauline to travel to visit him, so every day he would take up his fountain pen and write to her, unburdening his soul and sharing the torment he felt at being alive. Every day she would write back, urging him to stay strong, for the sake of his dead friends, and for her sake. For their future. After three months, Duncan was sent to Lowesby Hall RAF convalescent home, near Nottingham for a short period. On discharge from there, he was invalided out of the RAF as he was no longer fit for air crew duty. The loneliest day in his entire life was the one when he travelled back to Skellingthorpe to collect his belongings. His log book, his clothes, his bike, his old kit bag. They were all there. Drenched in memories. He was given a Demob suit, a hundred pounds and a disabled badge to prove that he was unfit for duty. Then he boarded a steam train bound for Manchester – and re-entered a world that had changed. For it was after D-Day.

While Duncan had been in hospital, on the night of June 5th, a thousand bomber raid by the RAF had targeted the coastal batteries of Normandy to prevent them from firing on the imminent invasion fleet – meanwhile the USAF had been in action over four of the Normandy landing beaches. Many months of planning and building-up a massive force of troops, had finally allowed the Allies to invade northern France. On June 6th, 1944 (known as D-Day) in an attempt to liberate Europe from Germany's occupying army, the greatest sea-borne invasion in history took place. Around one hundred and sixty thousand allied troops had embarked upon five thousand craft in southern England and landed on five beaches on the Normandy coast. They had been supported by thousands of aircraft, and further airborne landings behind the enemy lines.

When Duncan returned to Manchester in the autumn of 1944, the course of the war had only months to run. Paris had been liberated in the final week of August. The Allied forces of the USA, Britain, Canada, Australia and other Commonwealth countries were pushing across mainland Europe from the west, while the Soviets advanced from the east. It was almost over. The end of the war was anticipated by many and on May 7th 1945, a few weeks after Hitler's suicide in Berlin, Germany surrendered unconditionally. That afternoon at 3 o'clock, Winston Churchill broadcast to the British people. Loudspeakers were erected outside public buildings and crowds gathered in anticipation, while inside many homes families huddled around their wireless sets. Churchill's words brought the confirmation the nation wanted to hear – the war in Europe was over at last. "Hostilities will end officially at one minute after midnight to-night, but in the interests of saving lives the *Cease Fire* began yesterday to be sounded all along the front." Churchill's familiar voice echoed in every ear. "We may allow ourselves a brief period of rejoicing," he added to the listening millions.

The next day was declared VE Day – Victory in Europe. Coloured bunting, flags and ribbons were festooned everywhere. People began dancing in the streets, parties were hastily organised and celebration bonfires were lit. Bottles of sherry were removed from their dusty hiding places and enjoyed. There were balloons, streamers and party hats, and despite the severe rationing, parents managed to conjure up treats and party food for the children. In London, crowds converged on Buckingham Palace, cheering and waving Union Jacks, as the Royal Family appeared and then re-appeared again and again, on their famous balcony.

For Duncan and Pauline, VE day had dawned brightly, but they did not take part in any of the local celebrations as Duncan was still not fully recovered and thus unable to mix with crowds.

Together they listened to the wireless broadcasts, smiling at the descriptions of street parties, neither one wanting to break their tenuous happiness by calling up painful memories of absent friends. But in their minds were thoughts of the missing crew, and their hearts ached for those who would never taste the hard won freedom and joy. The freedom that was paid for with their forfeit lives.

And of course it wasn't over. The menace in the East still had to be quelled. At 8.15 on the morning of August 6th the end began, carried by a plane called Enola Gay. The initial yellow glow, then the blinding, overwhelming white flash, followed by red, then violet and then, only then, the mushroom cloud of no hope. Hiroshima was followed by Nagasaki. Japan surrendered unconditionally. The second war to have involved the entire world was at an end. Another "war to end all wars" was finally over. Surely nothing so terrible would ever happen again? Millions of people had lost their lives throughout the course of the war. Say it to yourself quietly first of all, let the sounds gently echo round your head. Then say those words out loud. Millions of people – men, women, children, babies, civilians, service personnel, volunteers, nurses, industrial workers, schoolchildren.

Simultaneously rejoicing and in shock, those who had survived gave thanks amid tears. The telegraph boy – the angel of death – would no longer come knocking, delivering his awful words. There would be no more telegrams. No more bombs. For now.

For Duncan (as for so many others), the end of the war brought the most bitter sweet pain. And it was laced with memories, with tears and with the desperate, crazed belief that he had no right to have survived. While for Pauline, the wild joy and utter relief at having Duncan by her side, was tempered by the overwhelming grief that she knew he was enduring. It was the cross he must bear.

But time moves on. Even the bitterest pain softens.

The initial post war delirium and joy felt by the general public was soon blurred by post war austerity. Rationing was still in force, with food, clothing and fuel in very short supply. The winter of 1945 was exceptionally severe and heating homes was almost impossible as coal was severely rationed. It was a difficult time. The major cities were ravaged with derelict bombsites and bomb damaged buildings. The reconstruction of Britain began slowly and all new building work was subject to very strict controls, as materials (especially timber) were very scarce.

When Duncan had more or less recovered from his dreadful illness, he was able to return to his former trade of joiner where his skills were much in demand. Manchester Corporation decided to begin their reconstruction project by replacing a few council houses that had been destroyed by bombs. A team of men, comprising two bricklayers, a young apprentice, two labourers and Duncan (as the carpenter) were given the task of rebuilding the very first new council houses – a pair of semi-detached homes in Burnage. A journalist and a photographer arrived at the building site one day, to get a story and snap a picture of the gang for posterity. The photo appeared in the *Manchester Evening News* and the men felt a certain pride in their fleeting fame. It was a long, slow struggle to rebuild the city, but as those who had survived returned from their war duties and took up their old skills again, the phoenix that was Manchester slowly began to rise from the ashes.

Time went by. One warm and golden September day in 1948, a gypsy, begging for food, knocked at the door of the little council house that Pauline and Duncan rented. Duncan had left early for work on his bike, and Pauline was alone. She was nervous, just a little afraid, of opening the door. But the gypsy had looked thin and frail – surely there was no danger. The woman had begged for a little jam to feed her children. Pauline couldn't resist the woman's pleas and thus her kindness earned a fortune telling.

"You don't have any children yet, do you?" the gypsy had enquired of Pauline.

"No" she had replied, cautiously, wondering if the woman was leading up to asking for more food.

"You will soon," smiled the gypsy. "And you'll have a boy, my dear," she added knowingly.

When Pauline had realised she was pregnant a few months later, she and Duncan had been overcome with joy. It would be a continuation – a new life – a reminder of those precious ones so recently lost. The gypsy's prophecy foretold that their child would be a boy. It seemed right, it was fitting. They considered a name for the child. The baby would be called Keith, in memory of Ben Lawrence (whose real name was, of course, Keith) and the rest of the crew.

It was a stifling hot June day when the baby entered the world. The last few weeks of June had been unbearable for Pauline, as an early heatwave had made her ponderous body feel even heavier. The sun beat down relentlessly, causing windows to be cast wide open, and allowed Pauline's agonised cries from the bedroom to pierce the air. Then there was quiet, and exhausted gasps of relief.

The child was born. A girl. Me.

Of course, my parents hadn't consider the possibility of a baby girl. The gypsy's prediction had seemed so right, so fitting. They had no female names picked out and ready. No Annabels, no Helens or Josephines ready to be bestowed on the tiny creature. My arrival made them realise that few things in life are predictable. Their quiet lives changed overnight. A healing process began and suddenly there was no room for dwelling on the past. Their child – the future – was everything. And so of course, life went on, just as it should.

All those dreadful sacrifices would have been for nothing, had it been otherwise. Forever young, forever brave, their brief sweet lives given for you – and for me.

And my father kept the solemn promise that he made.

Never forget.

Epitaph

My brief sweet life is over, my eyes no longer see,
No summer walks – no Christmas Trees – no pretty girls for me,
I've got the chop, I've had it, my nightly ops are done,
Yet, in another hundred years, I'll still be twenty-one.

by Ralph Wilson Gilbert, Mid-Upper Gunner

Bibliography & Acknowledgements

Campbell, James. *The Bombing of Nuremberg*. London: Allison and Busby Limited, 1973.

Middlebrook, Martin. *The Nuremberg Raid*. London: Allen Lane, 1973.

Searby, John. *The Bomber Battle for Berlin*. Shrewsbury, England: Airlife Publishing Limited, 1991.

Smith, Peter J. C. *Luftwaffe Over Manchester: The Blitz years*. Manchester: Neil Richardson, 2003.

http://www.rafbombercommand.com RAF Bomber Command website

Lancashire Aircraft Investigation Team (LAIT)
http://web.ukonline.co.uk/lait/site/Botha-Defiant.htm

Special thanks to Peter Moran and Russell Brown

History of Bobbington
http://www.chipmonk.demon.co.uk/bobbhome.htm. Special thanks to Brian Pitt

http://www.doramusic.com Information about Alan Blumlein

Finally, special thanks to all at the Lincolnshire Aviation Centre, East Kirkby, Lincolnshire.

My Father, Duncan.

My Mother, Pauline.

My pencil drawing of Agnes – the grandmother I never knew.